LIFE IN AN AIR-COND'

Michael Bantu-Khoe is the s,
twelve, originally from Botsw
and studied abroad, Michael t
in the United Kingdom. This b   ....., ms journey
and how he dealt with life's thorniest issues, including
losing a loved one during the COVID-19 pandemic,
coping with mental health illness, and combating the
depressingly persistent impact of racism and
discrimination.

In a David-versus-Goliath hostile environment, this
book documents a black man's lived experience in
modern-day Britain. Read on as he tells the good, the
bad, and the ugly, exposing both the highs and lows
through light-hearted humour. Michael's experience
sheds light on how black people often navigate a
strange and convoluted social structure, rigid with
shady practises that have been fostered since the
beginning of slavery. Fighting racism and overcoming
giants is no walk in the park. Even Achilles was only as
strong as his heel.

Dig in, if you will, to some of his fun (ish) childhood
stories that share a lot about the fun side of coming

MICHAEL BANTU-KHOE

from a large family and struggling with poverty. Meet his family and friends who played a crucial part in his life. They are the ones to whom this book is dedicated.

Life In An Air-Conditioned Hell

*A Memoir Full of Stories Of
The Sixth Born African Child
In A Family of Twelve*

MICHAEL BANTU-KHOE

First paperback edition March 2022

Book design by Michael Bantu-Khoe

ISBN 978-1-7397205-4-4 (Paperback)
ISBN 978-1-7397205-9-9 (Hardcover)
ISBN 978-1-7397205-2-0 (eBook)

Black O'clock Publishing LTD
86-90 Paul Street,
London, England,
United Kingdom,
C2A 4NE
www.blackoclock.com
www.michaelban2khoe.com

Ordering Information: Quantity sales. Exceptional discounts are available on quantity purchases by corporations, associations, and others. For details, contact the publisher at the address above. Orders by US/UK trade bookstores and wholesalers. Please contact Big Distribution via email: **info@blackoclock.com or visit**
www.blackoclock.com

MICHAEL BANTU-KHOE

LIFE IN AN AIR-CONDITIONED HELL

MICHAEL BANTU-KHOE

To my family, thank you for raising me into the man I am.

MICHAEL BANTU-KHOE

LIFE IN AN AIR-CONDITIONED HELL

MICHAEL BANTU-KHOE

CONTENTS

LIFE IN AN AIR-CONDITIONED HELL

MICHAEL BANTU-KHOE

THE WOMAN
WHO INSPIRES ME

MY MOTHER , ELVA

MICHAEL BANTU-KHOE

CHAPTER 1

"**B**ring her outside, you crazy, insane witch! I want my daughter! I'm certain she's in there somewhere. Otelia, please come on over, sweet girl. I promise not to harm you...Did you hear me? I swear I won't hurt you! Otelia 'Otelia! Otelia! " Those screams came from an enraged mother who stood at our front door, persistently buzzing through the intercom while shaking the locked steel rail gate incredibly hard in an effort to

MICHAEL BANTU-KHOE

break in. We were all going to die, I thought! I could see a furious throng assembled in front of our home, yelling and wielding clubs and tiki torches as I peered through the curtains.

"What exactly is going on here?" I carefully enquired of others who were nearby. Nobody said anything at first. I glanced at mum to see if she could explain what was going on, but she instead told me to keep away from the windows because it was not safe. "Why are there so many people crowding around our home?" I sobbed aloud. My elder sister, who was clearly becoming irritated with me, pushed me to the side and stated flatly, "That's Otelia's mum," she remarked, pointing to Otelia, and adding, "They're after her." They've come to take her back home.

As soon as Otelia heard what my sister said, she pleaded with my mother. "Please, please, please don't let them take me!" She implored my mother while clutching her skirt firmly and crying tears down her cheeks. My father was away on a business trip or a military assignment at the time. As a result, my mother was left to deal with the matter on her own, attempting to do what any loving parent or good Samaritan would have done in this situation.

Regardless, I believe it is reasonable to conclude that her altruistic actions this time put her and all of us in grave danger. To give you some context, Otelia had managed to flee her home. She showed up at our house three days before the mob, most likely in the dead of night. The poor child was significantly hurt, and she said that her parents had beaten her up mercilessly on a regular basis, prompting her to flee. She had been on the run for days without eating. When my mother pulled up to our house and noticed Otelia searching through our trash bins looking for leftover food, she called out to her.

My mother, being the kind Samaritan that she is, was compelled to nurse and care for Otelia after seeing her physically injured and wounded. It was at this point that Otelia confided to my mother, that she was a runaway kid who had been violently tortured by her parents. My mother then decided to let Otelia live with us for the time being, at least until things settled down and we figured out how to contact and engage the not-so reliable social services.

Otelia stank the place up as she walked in through our front door. I couldn't sit near her without coughing and sputtering at the rancid smell until she took a couple of baths. In addition, I'd never seen anybody eat so quickly or so much in my life. The situation worsened to the point that we all had to limit our breakfast, lunch, and supper quantities due to the new guest. As a direct consequence of this, many of my siblings and I developed a strong disdain for her at the time. We were obviously too young to care or even comprehend Otelia's awful situation. All we observed was someone breaking into our already crowded home and devouring all of our food.

My mother, on the other hand, was going about her business as usual. Which entails being overly concerned and, at any cost, seeking to care for the destitute and needy. That self-assurance is what drove her to go out and face an angry crowd of hundreds on her own. According to witnesses, my mother held firm and was seen having a furious debate with other members of the mob, nearly ready to take on the whole crowd by herself. Thankfully, it never came to that because the police got there just in time to stop things from escalating out of control. It wasn't long after they came that the masses dispersed, and our streets were clogged with police officers. That night, both my mother and Otelia's parents were detained. Otelia was carefully escorted into a different police vehicle parked in front of our home by two police officers who entered our house. I remember being delighted to see Otelia leave our home, but also sad and worried sick for my mother, since she was the last person I expected to be hauled away in handcuffs.

Fortunately, word got out that Otelia's parents were renowned among the authorities and social services for abusing and mistreating their children. How did they get away each time they got arrested? I do not know. My mother was released the following morning with no charges filed against her. In fact, she was called to testify against Otelia's parents in a different incident a few months later. Now that I think about it, I wish I had a heart as big as my mum's. It is only now, when I reflect on this episode, that I can realise what type of woman she is. Over the course of her life, she has made it her mission to care for disadvantaged children and adults, particularly those who are homeless. The best way to characterise my mother is to use a well-known proverb in my culture, that goes like this: *Mosadi ke thari ya Sechaba*, which means "A Woman is the cradle of the nation". Or rather, she is the bearer of the nation. I think the saying came from seeing a mother carry her baby on her back every day. That to me, epitomises how resilient my mother is.

I say resilience because, for as long as I can remember, the path of my mother's life has been anything but easy sailing; rather, it has been riddled with obstacles, challenges, struggles, and tribulations. She has always shown an incredible amount of resilience in the face of these difficulties. To give you a bit of a backstory, my mother has a total of twelve children that she has birthed over her life. So, in point of fact, she spent the better part of her precious adult life constantly nursing and changing diapers. Despite this, we were able to feel the love and care that she had for us. It was quite akin to the way a mother hen protects her young. Thanks to her, I am also now able to tell people that I am one of twelve or that I have eleven siblings from the same parents. There are five boys and seven girls, and I am sixth in the pecking order, in case you were wondering. Therefore, I am in a much better position to assess whether or not having a large family was a wise choice.

Interestingly, having a big family was very common in Africa, but having twelve children was unusual. We weren't exactly well-off; thinking back on my childhood, I grew up impoverished, to say the least, and became used to living a simple life. In terms of jobs and supporting us, my father served in the military as a solider, and my mother had to work two jobs, one as a salesperson at a furniture store and the other as a self-employed food caterer selling exquisite packed lunches — all of this hard work to augment my father's salary and pay our school tuition.

Unlike in the UK, where school education is free or affordable, in Botswana in the early 2000s, you had to pay school fees for your kid every term or risk having them expelled from school. And, depending on the location or level of school your kid attends, the fees may be substantial and deplete your monthly income.

MICHAEL BANTU-KHOE

Imagine having to budget for and pay for twelve children. She was extremely adept at managing our household finances and kept us afloat.

My mother embodies the term "hustler" in its purest form. She came from a single-parent family, and she was forced to drop out of school when she was young so that her brothers could get an education. She had to remain at home to assist her mother and save money on school fees for the family. As a result, my mother didn't go to school like she should have. Even so, she taught herself to read and write, and she is fluent in five languages. She tells me about how, as a teenager, she would sell prepared meals at the street market while carrying a basket full of fruits and vegetables. So young, she learned how to run a business, hustle, and make money to help support her family. Her brothers are now well educated, and some of them even have master's degrees and PhDs. My mother, on the other hand, doesn't have any qualifications. She never finished her GCSEs.

MICHAEL BANTU-KHOE

LIFE IN AN AIR-CONDITIONED HELL

MICHAEL BANTU-KHOE

THE TWELVE

DISCIPLES

MICHAEL BANTU-KHOE

CHAPTER

2

When family fights happen, no one f**ken wins. When my brother uttered those words, a part of me really wanted to yell back at him and say, "Shut the f*** up and let these people fight!" Instead, I chickened out and stood there with my hands over my head, watching my siblings calm down from their dispute to the point where they were practically making up and embracing each other like a shitshow.

MICHAEL BANTU-KHOE

I was definitely not a regular kid growing up. As a middle child, nothing piqued my interest more than a family feud, particularly sibling rivalry, which often erupted into violent altercations. I mean, it's entertaining to see your uncles (relatives) fight at a family barbeque every now and then, but it only occurred around Christmas and New Year's, and I wanted something more regular, if you know what I mean.

Even though I took a lot of beatings as a fighter in these sibling squabbles, my victories came only when I got to be a spectator on the side and kept score of the strikes and landed punches, as well as the number of knockouts throughout these fights. So now you know what made me so angry at my brother for breaking up the fight at my parents' house during what would turn out to be our last Christmas together. To remember the event, one of my siblings suggested that we take a family photo with all of us to commemorate our family. This, surprisingly, was something we've never done before in the history of our family. It never occurred to anyone of us that we might need a picture of us all together to frame it or something. When I think about it, I can't help but wonder why we haven't done this previously, especially when every other family appears to have theirs displayed in a photo frame. Well, as it so happens, a few valid arguments sprang to mind, one of which was the most apparent. There are just too many of us, and it is simply too much work! It's not like we're posing for the freshman year cover of XXL magazine. There was no incentive to have us all huddled together and flaunting our dreadful features.

Furthermore, having too many people results in far too many distractions. Have you ever asked a child to sit still for more than two minutes? Impossible. Even for adults, it is a big ask. I just can not maintain a grin for so long and appear to be okay with just doing that many retakes because a few people had their eyes closed or were caught chatting and moving. But no matter how hard you tried to get all of us in the picture, someone's legs, limbs, or head was always going to get cut off. This was the outcome of the photo we took. As you can see below, we just about managed to get everyone's face on it. It's a good thing we set everyone up like a football team, with the younger children up front and the older siblings at the back. Who knows, maybe one day we'll recreate the photo into a realistic painting in honour of our parents. However, for the time being, the new photo has been placed as the profile image for our WhatsApp family group.

The Family Portrait:
Mum and Dad with their twelve children (December 2009)

MICHAEL BANTU-KHOE

You see, as a close-knit family, we came to the conclusion that the best way for all twelve of us to connect with one another would be to create a WhatsApp group and call it "12 Disciples". In the group, there are no defined rules and regulations. You are free to come and go as you like, and we often interact every day to keep each other updated on what is going on in our personal lives. We can also use the platform to have important family meetings, vote on issues, and prolong our family battles. Yes, our WhatsApp family group provides a safe space for squabbling siblings to quarrel verbally, albeit good feuds ultimately deepen or enhance our bonds. They can be entertaining to watch, — especially if you skip the apoplectic messages and go straight for the voicemail messages. Some of the vocal notes pierce through to the core. It's as if you're watching a famous hip hop rap battle, only instead of rapping, they're messaging and leaving recorded voicemails on the WhatsApp group. Soon as you see three dots on the message box, you know something 's coming!

Sure there've been instances when things get stressful and disrespectful at times, causing individuals to leave the group. Nevertheless, a little bit of begging brings them back. There is always something going on, no matter what time of day it is, and whatever happens in the group remains in the group; that's the unwritten family rule. Although you may need to remind one or two people to keep things private when you make a remark or share sensitive information, it doesn't harm to include a warning that reads, "Please, please DO NOT post this on social media." (Just to be certain.)

In addition, there has been a fair amount of gossip, both good and bad. But, as the twelve members of the jury, what better way to pass the time than to judge other people? Needless to say, the ultimate function of the WhatsApp family group is to encourage and support one another in pursuing their own aspirations. In other words, the platform enables us to essentially brainstorm, collaborate, pitch, and test business ideas.

You see, because of our mother's tenacious spirit and business acumen, we all aspire to become self-made entrepreneurs who do well. To achieve this, we have tailor-made our group to serve us like the American TV show Shark Tank or the UK's Dragon's Den. Using this as a starting point, siblings have been able to connect, develop partnerships, obtain financing, and even start their own businesses! It's great practise when the rest of the group takes on the role of angel investors or dragons, providing unfiltered feedback and thoughts to prepare you for the real world of business.

But none of this matters when you have to deal with the real world, which requires you to interact socially with total strangers on a regular basis. When I initially began travelling and experiencing other cultures and making new friends all across the globe, I noticed that people had a distinct reaction when they found out that I had eleven siblings, all of whom came from the same mother. They seem to be completely oblivious to the weird, perplexed expressions on their faces. There is never a grin there. Instead, it closely resembles the expression you get when you gaze upwards into the clear blue sky and look directly at the sun without wearing sunglasses (disclaimer: do not try this at home). But just picture their expressions! People would approach me, make that expression, and then ask the question: "So, what was it like to grow up in a big family?"

MICHAEL BANTU-KHOE

Every time I heard that question, it threw me off. It made me feel uneasy since I assumed people were merely asking to make fun of me. But the reality is that I enjoyed myself. That being said, it's not something I'd advocate for someone beginning a family. When I look back at my childhood, I can't help but feel blessed whenever I think back on it. Imagine being in the same home with all of your family and friends at the same time. Every day felt like a party. We had hard days, but there were many more wonderful days. If there's anything I can compare it to? Have you ever seen Steve Martin's family comedy film, Cheaper by the Dozen? That movie, sprinkled with some hardcore poverty scenes, encapsulates what it was like to grow up at home.

If I had millions of pounds or dollars stashed away in the bank, I would fund an African production of that film based on my family. Or even portray it as a reality show similar to Keeping Up With The Kardashians, simply because we have a wealth of interesting content and entertaining anecdotes that will keep you on the edge of your seat and make you fall in love with our family.

MICHAEL BANTU-KHOE

One such recollection involves a chat between my mother and myself. She'll probably hit me over the head for saying this. But earlier in my childhood, when I was about nine or ten years old, I became irritated and fed up. I recall returning from school after being taunted about my family. I decided to confront the main source of the issue and express my feelings to my mother, who was reading the Bible in bed. I came in through the door, and without saying hello to anybody, I remarked, "Mum, may I ask what prompted you and Dad to choose to have twelve children?" Everyone I know at school is making fun of me, comparing us to a football team with me as a reserve or substitute player on the bench. " My mother's response was not what I had anticipated. She responded casually, as if I had asked her what she had for lunch.

Those friends of yours, son, have no idea what they're talking about. "God gave me instructions," she added. "He's the one who said I should have twelve children." Really?" I responded.
"Yes, really! "God assigned this mission to your father and me, and I aim to carry it out to the letter. "

"But, mama, are you certain that was God?" because no one else at church has twelve children. Our neighbours three houses down have the most, according to my count; they have six. That's almost half of us. "

This did not seem to have any effect on Mama at all. "Come here, come sit next to me, and I'll read you something from my Bible that will answer your question," she said. I moved in closer and observed her as she went back and forth between the pages of the Bible in an effort to find a certain passage of scripture. Then, after what seemed like an eternity, she came to a halt on a certain page and kept doing this thing with her finger, as if reading in braille.

"Aha!" She triumphantly shouted. "I found it." Could you please read Genesis 1:27–28 for me? Please read it loudly so that I can hear you. " I held the book up close to my eyes and began to read it. It was the verse in which God instructed Adam and Eve to reproduce and replenish the Earth. My mother took those words to heart and thought that it was her God-given mission to populate the Earth, and so we were born. That was a difficult pill to take for a ten-year-old hearing those words for the first time. Imagine not knowing whether to laugh or reason with your mum. I went into her room expecting to hear something like,

"Oh right, just because you keep asking, I'm sorry to break it to you, but you and the majority of your siblings were all mistakes."
We had no intention of having more than five children. I would have taken something like that on the chin. Don't get me wrong, I am not criticising my parents for having a big family. In my opinion, we may or may not have been the only huge family in the country; there may have been others. My parents were free to do anything they wanted. I'm simply giving my thoughts at the time, which brings me nicely to my next revelation.

Growing up in Botswana, I was perplexed by a common practise among many Batswana, which helps to understand my parents' perspective. Money is never an impediment to having children, no matter how impoverished one is. My parents did not have enough money to support a large family. Don't get me wrong: we were mostly content, but as I already said, I wouldn't recommend it.

MICHAEL BANTU-KHOE

Later in life, I came to appreciate the second reason why my parents chose to have a big family. 2008 was the year I departed for university. Like the majority of 18-year-olds, I had no idea what I wanted to accomplish with my life. I had no idea what profession I wanted to pursue. Fortunately, this was already determined for me or set in stone. I was informed that I would become an architect like my grandpa. My mother made it seem like it was my fate or, in some ways, my life's mission. She sold me the dream, and I just bought into it. Honestly, I wasn't very enthusiastic about architecture. Considering the buildings in my neighbourhood, I saw them as mundane and utilitarian. I often questioned why anybody would want to work in that field for the rest of their lives. On the other hand, my mum told me she was extremely proud of me and that one day I would be the finest architect in the village. She is an excellent mother. She instilled in me the importance of self-confidence and the mindset that success was inevitable. As a result of her unshakable confidence in me, I began to believe in myself, which was empowering.

Likewise, on the surface, it seemed as if everyone of my eleven siblings had been given a career chance to pursue as well. You become a doctor, architect, lawyer, accountant, television director, fashion designer, marketing manager, or any number of other professions. But, in retrospect, Mum and Dad were being cautious. Both of my parents knew better than to put all of their eggs in one basket. They were diversifying their portfolio in the way that would be expected of a savvy investor in the game of life.

Truthfully speaking, part of the reason some African families have a large number of children is because their children grow up and have diverse careers and occupations. If one investment fails, the other will make up for the loss. If the fashion designer's clothing fails to sell, the nurse with a steady salary will step in. As the parents become elderly and need care, they will delve into their children's pockets and enjoy the benefits of their investment. This, my friend, is what is commonly referred to as the Black Tax. Rather astute, don't you think? To my parents, it was, and still is, a terrific retirement plan. Not so much, though, for the children who find themselves trapped in this never-ending cycle of debt. You repay what is owed to your parents until death do you part. I once overheard my mother and elder brother arguing. I believe he was grumbling about having to give them his hard-earned money on a monthly basis. He was fed up with the fact that he could not enjoy the fruits of his labour and wanted to take a sabbatical. My mother did not hesitate to put him in his place.

To this day, each and every one of us is still making payments into the "Bank of Mum and Dad." We are also patiently waiting for one of us to amass sufficient wealth to assume the responsibility or shoulder the load of freeing the others from their shackles and setting them free. Now, I don't want you to think badly of my parents' "pyramid scheme". But unfortunately, it is not just our household under the curse. The majority of families in Botswana and the rest of Africa run the same system in some shape or form.

While mom is typically the enforcer of the Black Tax norm in our home, dad is also a benefactor, albeit in a more polite and diplomatic manner than brutal. And that pretty much sums up Dad, although I struggled at times to characterise his personality. The father I know today is nothing like the one I grew up with. When I was growing up, my dad was a member of the armed forces and served in the military. He retired in his sixties and now lives in Botswana on his pension. He cannot get enough of the countryside and spends much of his time herding livestock and tilling the soil. Dad would take us out to the ranch or the cattle farm and tell us about the countryside lifestyle. He grew up drinking river water, hunting meat, and spending his childhood years living in mud huts where there were nightly campfires with the sound of roaring lions in the background. That's how my dad describes having a good time. He is the only man I know who still believes he can discover subterranean water simply by strolling around with a stick, and also believes that your tonsils can be cured by using a teaspoon dipped in chilly powder.

Despite his old methods, I give him credit because I still continue to use some of his brilliant ideas and insightful concepts that he developed. For example, despite being a lousy cook with a very low culinary or food IQ, I take solace in the knowledge that my father taught me this one basic way to remove the acrid scent from burned food. I learned this the hard way, so please feel free to take notes. One day, it was my turn to cook supper for the family, so I decided to make one of my all-time favourites: an African beef stew accompanied by a dish that we call "Pap," which oddly also means "dad," but in the context of food, it is just pounded cornmeal (or maize meal). When it is ready, it looks like white polenta. So, I cooked the meal in a traditional three-legged pot over an open fire outside while alternating between the outdoor kitchen and the interior kitchen, where I was preparing the beef stew.

Something strange occurred while I was cooking, and I became preoccupied, resulting in the burning of the beef stew. Fortunately, Dad was close. The smell of burning food was palpable. As soon as he entered the kitchen, he removed the cover from the pot that was on fire and added a little less than a quarter of a cup of water to the contents of the pot. After smacking me on the head, he urged me to pay attention as he inserted an enamel mug upside down inside the beef stew pot and replaced the lid. Approximately three to four minutes later, he lifted the lid and pulled out the enamel cup, which had absorbed the smell of the burnt food. Dad went through the procedure many times until he was satisfied with the way it smelled and tasted. Since that time, I have tried the experiment several times, and each time it has been successful for me.

However, the most important thing is to respond as fast as you can; if you don't, the pungent flavour may remain in your meal. To the best of my knowledge, the same method may be used to rescue burned gravy, sauce, or curry. In retrospect, I am quite pleased that my father taught us all of these skills, such as how to repair the electrics in the house, how to change a tyre securely, and, believe it or not, how to butcher a cow or goat for food. He was the Master of Agriculture, a devoted farmer who took great pleasure in taking care of all of his animals, which included a large number of sheep, goats, and calves. My father has a cow collection, in contrast to the vehicle collections that other people have.

The one and only drawback to this is that, in the end, it turned out to be nothing more than a pastime rather than a means to a goal. The cattle farm that my dad owns is, unfortunately, situated in a region that is now experiencing an outbreak of foot and mouth disease.

MICHAEL BANTU-KHOE

For fear of an epidemic, domestic animals used for meat cannot be slaughtered and sold to the general public. In order for my father to sell his cattle, they need to be given a specific treatment or vaccinated, both of which are rather expensive and impracticable, particularly when one is attempting to provide for a big family struggling to survive. Regardless, he remained a cow enthusiast. To top it all off, there are more cows in Botswana than people. It's no surprise he had so many. He's been stockpiling a lot of them.

The other aspect of my father that I became familiar with while I was growing up was somewhat sweeter. He suffered from PTSD—Post Traumatic Stress Disorder—as a result of his many years of service in the military. You don't want to run across him while he's having a terrible day, since his mood may shift in an instant. On a good day, though, he enjoys imparting knowledge and recounting anecdotes of near-death experiences, such as being ambushed by attackers or being thrown out of an aircraft flying 15,000 feet in the air with no experience of deploying a parachute. My dad is a fantastic storyteller. With his amusing sound effects, he personifies storytelling and role-playing. It

MICHAEL BANTU-KHOE

was like music to my ears when Dad chortled to himself before cracking a joke. He attempted to make every word of the joke humorous, even in the midst of it. Those nights, when dad would amuse us, are ones that I mourn deeply and long for.

Another thing I remember is that when I was a youngster, my dad used to trim my hair with scissors since we couldn't afford hair clippers or a trip to the barbershop. Dad had everything under control. After cutting the hair of twelve children with scissors, you'd think he'd have honed his talents to equal Nick Cannon's character in the film Drumline. But our hairstyles were far from satisfactory. When it was my time for a haircut, I used to cry my eyes out.

To win me over without having to wrestle and pin me down to the chair, Dad would sneak up to our room early in the morning and carefully start cutting my hair while I was still sleeping. I'd wake up in his arms to the snip-snip sound, only to discover that he was almost halfway finished. In that sense, I felt trapped because it was either go to school with one side of your hair gone or give in and endure while he finished off the other side of your head. But hey, it was my childhood, even though I still find it hard to accept it!

LIFE IN AN AIR-CONDITIONED HELL

MICHAEL BANTU-KHOE

HOME IS WHERE THE HEART IS

MICHAEL BANTU-KHOE

As you walk along a bustling city street in Botswana, you will notice a spectrum of skin tones, ranging from the deepest black to the palest white. Over the cacophony of traffic, you can hear snippets of dialogue in a multitude of languages. Towering office buildings shade you from the scorching heat as you make your way past vendors of fruit, souvenirs, and

MICHAEL BANTU-KHOE

apparel. I was born in this city, known as Francistown. It is the second biggest city in Botswana, often referred to by the locals as' The Ghetto'. The homeland and capital of the Bakalanga tribe, to which my mother belongs.

I feel really proud to have been born and raised in Francistown. It was at Nyangabgwe Hospital on the 4th of December 1989 that I came into this world. My parents didn't know what to name me at the time of my birth. According to mum, I remained nameless. The doctors and nurses who delivered me left a blank space to give my parents time to think of a name. They couldn't agree, so they asked the nurses for recommendations. Baby no-name lay there while ideas were bounced around. Finally, a nurse suggested Michael. This was during the time when Michael Jackson's Bad album was creating a buzz in Southern Africa, and it was cool to be a 'Michael'. I am so glad they picked that name for me because my parents had far worse alternatives for me, which I will delve into now. I will start with dad's choices because Mum's suggestions were the worst.

Dad believed in using Setswana names with somewhat prophetic meanings. So, according to him, he wanted to name me "Chabadimaketsi" because, moments before I was born, a madman dressed up in old shanty clothes appeared at his workplace, announcing to the public that my mother was giving birth to me at that very moment. They discovered it was true from multiple reliable sources; after all, how else could a madman have known? It's not like they had cellphones back then. So, dad wanted to give me that name because that's what the madman insisted I should be called— Chabadimaketsi, a name that can mean a person who amuses the crowd, a crowd-pleaser, or a national comedian. For the record, I would have loved that name, but it was way too long. Add that to my last name, and we would have reached all 26 letters of the alphabet. It's a good thing my mum stubbornly refused to go with that moniker.

All Setswana names have special and sometimes hilariously funny meanings. It is customary, for example, to name your first child Wantlha, which means "number one" in English. The second child may also be called Wabobedi, which means' number two', and Waboraro means' child 'number three'. Now, I won't continue with the counting because you get the point. In my culture, naming a kid is as easy as one, two, three. This is why I don't understand why my parents made naming me seem so difficult. I've included a list of my siblings in chronological order, with their names translated into English, below.

Boitumelo, meaning *happiness*
Tebogo, meaning *thankful*
Thabiso, meaning *bringer of joy*
Thabo, meaning *happiness or joy*
Keabetswe, meaning *I am given*
Michael *?????*
Khumo, meaning *riches*
Lorato, meaning *love*
Phenyo, meaning *victory*
Neo, meaning *God's gift*
Thato, meaning *God's will*
Lesedi, meaning *God's light*

As you can see from the list, the name Michael, which my parents gave me, deviates from the norm. It makes me feel like I was adopted and not related by blood.

MICHAEL BANTU-KHOE

However, you may learn about our family history by just looking at and reading the meanings of our names. The first batch seems to have been born at some of my family's best and happiest times. My mother had a gorgeous afro back then; she was full of energy, vibrant, and gregarious. She managed her own private restaurant, "semausu," a Setswana term for a small convenience shop or food stand similar to what street hawkers do. Customers queued up in droves to purchase lunch and dinner from her. Mum was a fantastic entrepreneur and a natural-born hustler, so we were never short on cash.

My father was a high-ranking officer in the military. It was unheard of in our community when both of my parents could afford to purchase their own automobiles, but they did. When we resided in the BDF Donga, which was a military housing camp for the Botswana Defence Forces, at one time there were only two households total that had a black and white television. Ours was one of those families. The fact that my parents had amassed some money is a contributing factor that helps to explain the name trend. However, immediately after my younger brother Khumo was born, the names started to change. They became more religious and spiritually inclined; it seemed like a cry for help to God. From 1993 onwards, the winds of change started to blow. From that point on, my parents struggled financially and experienced economic hardship. There was just too much competition in the fast-food industry. That impacted mum's business, leaving us with a single income from dad, which in itself wasn't enough to support a growing family.

Eventually, mum's dream restaurant went under, and we were forced to sell whatever was left of the business and move from the city to a village hundreds of miles away, where we could afford to live on a low income. Life in the village was much quieter, and the only way out was to seek deliverance from God. Later, attending church became mandatory. Mum was listening to the radio in the hospital bed the night before I was born. She was following a news report about a civil war that erupted in Liberia when rebels entered through the Republic of Côte d'Ivoire with the intention of capturing Liberian President Samuel Doe. Mum, perhaps under the influence of morphine and the pressure of finding a name for me before I showed up, decided to go with

Doe. Yep. Doe is my alternative middle name, although it is not an official one. It became my moniker, and Mum used it anytime she was upset with me. Because I detested this moniker, my siblings began using it to get back at me whenever we fought. I should have been wiser and kept my dislike of the name to myself. However, you live and learn.

I liked being called Michael at school. When I was alone with my father, he called me Thuso, but my mother called me Doe. As you can imagine, I was a confused child. I wish I had met the nurse who recommended my name be Michael. I'd give her loads of hugs for saving my life. I am the only kid in the family who has an official government English name on my birth certificate. It's a mistake my parents can't undo. I suppose that they were too preoccupied with the art of making children and not thinking about meaningful names to give us.

On average, the age gap between the children in my family is about a year or two. In all honesty, I don't know how mum managed to keep up with it. I have always thought of childbirth as a painful experience for women, albeit rewarding in the end. Mum made it look easy. I could also imagine the pressure weighing on my dad, as the head of the family, having to provide for a family that kept increasing year by year. That must have been a lot to juggle, but on the plus side, it saved them from having to buy a new set of clothes every so often. Before my younger siblings arrived, I was the last-born and the most adored, treasured, and indulged little child. My elder siblings have expressed their displeasure with the amount of attention my parents lavished on me. My siblings, in fact, got into a lot of problems as a result of me. In African homes, older siblings often babysit the younger siblings while their parents are at work. They'd get a pat on the back if they did a good job looking after you. If they didn't do a good job, they received a hefty slap across the face. When my younger siblings arrived, I experienced the same thing. It's simply a normal part of our family life.

Having said that, I don't necessarily blame my older siblings for having such feelings. To put it bluntly, I think it's really challenging for parents to show the same amount of love and affection to each of their children. It gets more difficult as the number of children grows. As a parent, you may be able to supply all of them with physical and material goods, but there will always be a lack of emotional connection. Although many parents frown upon addressing this issue, favouritism does occur in big families. There will always be the favourite kid and the least favourite kid. This is covered in the Bible as well. Who was Jacob's favourite among his twelve sons? Joseph was the one. Even among Jesus Christ's twelve apostles, John was his favourite. So it's not surprising that I've had this experience.

As a middle child, you already know that I stand no chance in the pecking order. I have what they call the middle child syndrome. I often had the impression that nobody paid any attention to me and that I had been forgotten about. My parents continued to adore me even after the birth of my younger brothers and sisters, but it was different than it had been in the past. To return to the slur that was hurled at me by some of the students who bullied me at school: If it were true that my big family is the size of a football (soccer) team, it would imply that as the middle child, I was destined to play the part of the player wearing the number 6 jersey and whose role it is to play in the centre of the field. This player often serves as the team captain and directs the plays, including passes and movement, for the whole squad. Everyone pays attention to him and follows his directions. I often wonder whether that was the part I was born to play. If that's the case, my character has betrayed me horribly. I do not fit the description given above. My opinion doesn't count for much in my family since, if we're being honest, there are many more fascinating and captivating personalities in our midst than there are in me. I won't mention names, but you'll figure out who mother and father's favourites are as you read. As a mild-mannered middle child, I seldom have the ability to persuade an audience to accept my point of view on subjects. I can't recall ever getting things done my way. Maybe I should study how to be a diplomat.

LIFE IN AN AIR-CONDITIONED HELL

MICHAEL BANTU-KHOE

X.Y.Z

EXAMINE

YOUR ZIP

MICHAEL BANTU-KHOE

Superheroes are only as powerful as their weaknesses, according to an article published on Screen Rant by writer Jared Canfield. While most of these supernatural beings focus on what they can do to rescue the world, their flaws and vulnerabilities come as a surprise and make them the laughingstock of the comedic world. The narrative would not be nearly as captivating if this were not included. Exploring each superhero's flaws, on the other hand, may be thrilling. I, on the other hand, spent a good portion of my childhood under the impression that I was some kind of superhero, at least to my neighbourhood buddies. My abilities mirrored those of a so-called American Ninja Warrior, thanks to the mix of anime and live-action martial arts films that I consumed at the time. I even understood at that age that great power comes with great responsibility, so if we kids played street football and someone else ended up kicking the ball up to the point where it got caught on the house roof, I was the hero who made his way up the house building to take the ball down and salvage the game.

Others would give it a go, but none of them would be as successful as I was. I would climb the tree adjacent to the house where the ball had been lodged before pouncing and clinging like a Kuala bear onto the roof gutters and making my way up. When I finally made it to the peak of the building, I would proudly raise both of my hands in the air like a champion, as if to declare that I had completed the mission. This would often elicit a jovial reaction from my friends, who were staring up at me from the ground below. After I had retrieved the ball, I would leap from the roof and land on both feet, acting as if I were flying like Superman. With the number of times I sprained my ankle doing that, you'd think I'd wind up wounded and in a wheelchair. But there was no stopping me! I was a superhero without an Achilles' heel. Actually, that's a complete fabrication. My days of being a neighbourhood superhero were cut short by a tragic incident that not only cost me my street cred but also landed me in a hospital, a place that I dread. Just as some individuals are terrified of clowns, one of my worst fears or phobias is being stuck inside a hospital.

Yes, the "hospital" cripples me the same way Superman is crippled by kryptonite. Simply put, it is the least pleasurable place for me, and I will explain why. I hate the peculiar smell of death and bodily fluids masked with disinfectant. No matter how much I care about someone, I find it difficult to go see them in the hospital. I just can't do it. This extreme phobia, however, did not occur by happenstance. My whole life, I have always connected the worst things that have happened to me with hospitals. For instance, my uncle once went into a hospital and never came out alive! Also, when I was ordered to defecate in a plastic cup so that the doctors could check for worms. Yeah, I was the thinnest kid ever, and no matter how much I ate, I never appeared to put on any weight. What about the time when the doctor initially told my mother about the "Child Enema Pump" (Spati as we call it in Setswana), which provides fast constipation relief treatment for children who are unable to poo? I despised that thing; it brought out the worst in me, no pun intended.

In light of this, I wish I had a time machine to enable me to go back in time and prevent myself from making the choice that resulted in my hospitalisation and relinquishing my playtime with friends. I was maybe seven or eight years old at the time. My day got off to a great start as I walked outside to play Kung Fu with my younger brother and other youngsters from our neighbourhood. Karate exhibitions are only impressive to watch on television. We, on the other hand, were disorganised and scattered everywhere. I recall us emanating the confidence of ninjas wielding nunchakus. We'd yell "Kiai, Kai, Kai," over and over again. synchronising the sound of our voices with an aggressive killer move and a threatening gaze. Imitating the many characters from martial arts movies like Bruce Lee, Jackie Chan, Jet Li, and Michael Dudikoof. I was kicking ass while wearing denim pants for the silliest of reasons. I'm still not sure why I opted to wear them, but they're the reason I ended up in the hospital. I have nothing against jeans; I believe they are a remarkable invention. One of my all-time favourite classic R'n'B tunes is "In Those Jeans" by an artist called Ginuwine. So yes, I like jeans; I'm just not a massive fan because of what occurred afterwards.

So, I decided to take a toilet break for a pee. To be clear, I blame my habitat in part for what was about to happen. See, unlike in the rich suburbs, an indoor toilet in my neighbourhood was a luxury that poor people could not afford. As a little boy, you could get away with finding a tree and doing your thing in privacy. If you urgently needed to do a number two on the spot and just couldn't hold it in any longer, the same rule of thumb applied. When you'd already been playing outdoors and weren't near enough to your house to use an outhouse or pit toilet, your only options were as follows:

Option One: You either poop your pants (I can't believe I'm saying that) and be courageous enough to face being laughed at by your friends, or you risk being smacked on the bottom by your parents when you get home. Or you could go with Option Two, which involves the possibility, although a remote one, that you might avoid all of the fuss and empty your bowels the caveman way. Essentially, it is an old-school technique that enables Mother Nature to take care of you.

Therefore, if you find yourself in a precarious scenario in which your bottom is literally about to explode, the first thing you think about is location, location, location. I can't emphasise how crucial it is to locate a secluded and pleasant area in the bushes where you can dig a hole in the ground and relieve yourself. Look, I've done this before, so I'm not asking you to do anything I haven't done myself. But I know exactly what I'm talking about. There may be times when you will be caught off guard and find yourself without toilet paper, a handful of fast-food napkins, or even anything as soft as an old newspaper to wipe yourself with after doing your business.

So, if it ever occurs to you and you find yourself in that predicament, don't worry. Maintain your cool. I may have a few things up my sleeve to assist your stupid ass. By the way, the advice I'll be giving is not confined to a select few. In fact, if I were you, rich or poor, I would be taking notes. If the COVID-19 epidemic has taught us anything, it is that toilet paper is worth its weight in gold. You cannot risk going through a panic-buying period, causing toilet paper shortages at every retail shop in town. I'm not sure what it is, but it seems to me that running out of toilet paper is simply a fear people have in the back of their minds.

Therefore, if you ever run out of it but have to make an emergency stop, adhere to the measures I've outlined. And if it is safe to do so, use primitive techniques. However, once you reach your conclusion, remember to bury your faeces. You do not want someone to tread on your faeces. The last phase involves searching for a patch of sand and lowering your filthy behind to the ground in the same manner as an aeroplane landing on a runway. Do that with your bum, and at the end of the runway, pick yourself up and dust yourself off. Besides the smell, you should be as good as clean. I have put up a picture to illustrate how the ground should look after you have landed.

But, again, I digress. Let us return to our narrative. What was I talking about? The playground, of course. So I took a break from karate-chopping to urinate beside a nearby mopane tree. Of course, as an adult, I would never consider doing anything like that. However, as a child, I regarded it as just watering the plants with my fresh pee. So, as I was finishing up, I did that thing where you bend forward to tuck in... um... your willie. I wasn't paying full attention while doing it, and by the time I tied up my flies, the teeth had already been entangled in the foreskin! I completely lost it and yelled, "Argh!" like a small child. In all candour, I shrieked so loudly that the whole of the neighbourhood had to have been able to hear me. I don't think I've ever yelled at such a high volume in my whole life. It seemed as if everything was taking place in slow motion. It was the most agonising ache I have ever experienced in my whole life. I bolted for my home as fast as I could, my fists clenched tightly and glued to my crotch. I was gripping the shattered package as firmly as I could.

A few other street boys saw what happened, and I could see them telling one another, followed by an outburst of laughter. Still running in pain, as I made a turn to our street, I turned my head back to gauge their reaction, and they were literally pissing themselves, bent over laughing hysterically. I think it is safe to say that this day marked the end of my street credibility.

When I arrived at the house, I told my older brothers what had happened. They first assumed I was kidding until I showed them the damaged goods. One of them tried to remove the zip, but as he pulled, the zip's teeth dug deeper into my foreskin. Believe me when I say there are no other words in the English language that can completely explain the anguish I experienced. I was weeping uncontrollably because there was blood everywhere. My brother, the self-appointed nurse, became annoyed with me and smacked me to get me to stop weeping and remain still. That, however, gave me even more cause to cry even louder.

Not long after that, mum and dad arrived, with everyone staring at my dangling willy entangled in the zip as if I'd just had a terrible piercing. They eventually obtained a pair of scissors. No, they did not sever my penis, you pricks! Instead, they began cutting through my jeans to relieve me of my misery. That lone pair of jeans was the only one in my closet. I was half-naked, covered in a towel, and still bleeding, while everyone around me spoke to me and tried to calm me down. Finally, my dad came to get me, buckled me into his car, and off we drove to the hospital where I was born.

I was in such a state of panic when we got to the emergency ward that they placed me on a bed as soon as we got there. Because of my phobia of hospitals, the smell and fear of death got to me. I threw a temper tantrum of epic proportions, and things quickly spiralled out of control. The medical staff made many attempts to immobilise me and secure me to the bed, but they were unsuccessful. I think the adrenaline surge caused me to resist to the point that I accidently punched one of the female nurses in the boobs. The unfortunate woman had to take a seat and place a call for extra support. Finally, the doctor administered a sedative injection to me. I grew weak and restless till I passed out.

I remember waking up to a bustle, as if I were continuing to pick up where we left off in the fighting scene, only to discover a part of my manhood covered and wrapped in bandages. Mum and dad, who were meant to be sitting beside me, were nowhere to be seen. It seemed that the doctors had informed them that I would be OK and that they may go home. I mean, I get that it was late at night and they were exhausted and all. Even so, who abandons their child in the hospital?

So, yeah, I was circumcised that day, which was, in my perspective, a horrible solution to the issue. I really hope I could still file a lawsuit against the hospital for this; I didn't want to lose my foreskin in such a horrible way. But, alas, it was taken away from me, and as a result, I now feel as if a piece of me is missing. And the thing that I've always wanted to ask, is what do they do with the foreskins that they collect from patients? Do they discard them? Do they keep or sell them? Do they recycle the skin and reuse it to manufacture belts and other unknown leather products? I'm simply curious. Please let me know if you work in the forensic autopsy unit and know what happened to my foreskin. With much appreciation.

When I woke up the next morning, I had a million questions. I recall being disgusted by my genitalia in particular. Despite feeling numb, I continued rubbing the edges because they were itchy. If you've ever had a plaster cast put on, you'll understand how I feel. I recall fretting and wondering whether the surgeons had severed my willy. And if they had, what would I do next? Would it grow back? Would I be getting a new one? In the meantime, how would I pee? Did I need to pee right now? I was quite stressed. Needless to say, this whole incident made me hate the hospital even more.

Even today, whenever there is a family gathering, someone will invariably bring up the "penis incident," and everyone will burst out laughing, each with their own rib-cracking take on the story. And all the while, I'm making a fool of myself by attempting to downplay everything and defend myself when, in reality, I'm just making everything worse. I'm adding more gasoline to the fire.

To be honest, I grew up in a family full of bullies, and their continual tormenting motivated me to outwit them. One day, I thought enough was enough. I needed to put on my Sherlock Holmes hat and conduct some investigation work if I was going to stand up for myself. So I began digging up dirt on my siblings in order to keep them from talking about my ordeal. For self-defence, I blackmailed them into silence. I had to think outside the box and listen in on conversations to gather information I could use against them. When I discovered anything really beneficial, I would scribble it down on a scrap of paper and keep it safe. I probably had more evidence than the Biggie and Tupac murder cases in about a month or two.

I now had ammunition to use against my siblings the next time they attempted to humiliate me with the penis joke. I was ready, and I wasn't reluctant to snitch! For example, I knew I could rat on my sister for using Mom's Tupperware, which was a death penalty in itself. Or I might inform my dad where my brothers stashed their hoard of adult entertainment magazines. Or maybe tell my parents about how one of my siblings faked my mother's signature on one of their school reports. All of these secrets made me feel untouchable. At least, that's what I thought.

But then another zip-like experience occurred to me. This time was worse and more terrible than the previous since I should've known better. And how my siblings found out is a mystery to me to this day. I no longer had the upper hand after this shocking episode. Here's why I feel the encounter was both embarrassing and pleasurable. It all started when I was around 16 years old at the time, sitting in a classroom full of year 11s (Form 3), only a few months before my school GCSEs. Puberty decided to pay me a visit, which surprised me since I've always been a late bloomer. While other students battled acne and boasted about their pubic hair, I went through school unscathed until one day I'd rather forget.

While in detention one afternoon, I took a lengthy snooze at my desk. I was happy since I had a window seat. Despite not knowing the giant guy behind me (who was undoubtedly the alpha male in the room) or the tomboyish girl to my left, I felt at ease. It had been a long afternoon, lasting around three hours, so I knew I was in for some much-needed rest.

The last thing that was on my mind before I drifted off into dreamland was how pleasant the warm sunlight felt on my lap from the sun shining in through the window. I went straight from that thought to the next, while in REM sleep, which is rapid eye movement sleep that causes vivid dreams. I was fully spaced out, and it felt pretty good, but maybe a bit too good in this instance. I woke up in the middle of a dream that was too vivid even for this book, but let's just say it was too weird to tell you all that was going on. I woke up in the middle of a very detailed dream—even more so than is necessary for this book—but let's just say it was too weird for me to be able to describe it to you in full detail. But I'm willing to skim through so you don't lose out on too much. In a nutshell, we are all aware that the connection between the mind and the body is a strange one. With that in mind, I had a wet dream in the middle of the day at school.

When I woke up, I realised I had chosen the wrong day to not wear underwear with these khaki pants. It was as if I had spilt a half glass of water on my lap, just next to my sausage. So I sat there with a tennis ball-sized splotch on the front of my pants. And, as you can imagine, I was completely embarrassed. Not so much of the very visible and obvious outcome I'd left on my lap. But since I woke up exactly at the climax, I had no idea who I was or where I was.

A lot of thoughts and questions have plagued me since that fateful day. I think about the students who sat next to me and wonder whether they saw me gyrating and moaning in my seat. Was I yelling? I need to know whether I was playing out the sexy dream in detail and if any sound effects were used. Can you imagine if something occurred and someone recorded it and then put it on the internet? I would have been well-known for all the wrong reasons. Oh, how I wish I could erase this memory forever. All I know is that the following half hour of detention was the strangest and most awkward period I've ever spent in a classroom. I also had to pretend to study a scientific textbook over my "spill," hoping that the sun's warm rays would dry it up. When the sky suddenly became gloomy, that beam of optimism quickly vanished. And just as the school bell rang to end the day, I was thinking of new ways to hide what I had done wrong.

But unfortunately, I didn't have anything to cover it with. I was certain that if I was caught, I would be the target of scorn for years. Sadly, an unfortunate girl I knew had gone through something similar a few months before. She got her period for the first time in a classroom full of students. The whole school made fun of and bullied the poor girl. The bloodstains on the back of her skirt were visible as she went along the hallway. Students yelled and mocked her. Unfortunately, she was tormented throughout the remainder of her stay at that school. I was certain I'd go through the same ordeal if the word spread.

So, what exactly did I do? I tried my hardest to remain calm. I lingered behind after the school bell rang and waited until everyone had exited the classroom. When the detention teacher arrived, I feigned to be unwell with food poisoning, making it difficult for me to move due to severe stomach pains. For some reason, the teacher believed me and sent one of the pupils loitering near the locker room to get the school nurse. When the school nurse arrived, she was glad to stay and do tests on me with her medical kit. The teacher then left me in her care. I kept glancing aside when it was just the two of us, hoping she wouldn't see the patch. Unfortunately, she could not only see it, but she could also smell it.

You know how when you have horrible breath, a foul stench, or even just farted in front of a stranger, you become hyper-vigilant and keep convincing yourself that the other person must certainly smell it? They may not smell anything bad or exhibit any emotion, but you are certain they are aware that you let one fly. That is precisely what happened to me that day. I felt obligated to come clean since I feared the nurse could smell the strong odour of sperm. I informed her I wasn't unwell and was merely acting sick for the reasons stated above. Surprisingly, she merely shrugged her shoulders and grinned, as if there was nothing to be embarrassed or guilty of. The nurse handed me some Kleenex and promised to keep our little secret between us.

Finally, I left the school grounds with a dried patch, and no one noticed. I walked with an extra bounce in my step, as though doing a victory lap. I kept on telling myself that I would carry this experience with me to the grave without a doubt. I had no idea that the nurse to whom I confessed my sins was the girlfriend of my mother's brother's nephew's cousin's former roommate. And, sure, that's how my little secret made its way to the ears of my oppressors, a.k.a. my family.

MICHAEL BANTU-KHOE

TWELVE KIDS
IN A TWO BED
BUNGALOW

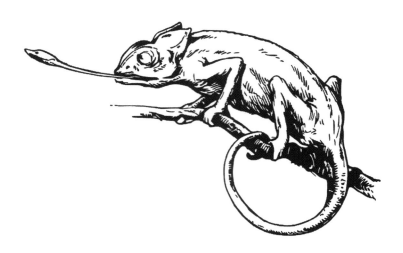

MICHAEL BANTU-KHOE

CHAPTER

5

Moving from the bustling metropolis of Francistown to the rural and secluded community of Maun was not without its share of hardship. Dad, who was still in the military, was presented with two transfer options: he could move to Gaborone City and enjoy the affluent life there. Another option would be for him to move to Maun village, where the town centre looked nothing like it does now. In those days, you didn't have to go very far to see traditional mud huts, broad unpaved roads, and domestic animals freely roaming the neighbourhood. Dad wanted us all to be closer to our grandparents in Maun.

I will never forget how difficult it was for me to say goodbye to our previous neighbourhood and the friends we had made there. When we arrived at Maun, we found that it was not what any of us had anticipated, or at least not the children. The fact that the house was only forty percent finished wasn't disclosed to us by our parents. They were aware of this the whole time, but I think they felt it would be better for us to relocate first and then notify them when we got there. That way, we wouldn't be able to alter their minds or reverse their decision. As a result, we were duped into relocating to Maun.

Our first mistake was moving into our grandparents' home. What began as a brief stay of a few days turned into several weeks and, finally, a couple of months. My grandparents lived in a two-bedroom house with an outhouse. Because we had grown up in a more developed town, our living standards and expectations were slightly higher than those of the people in Maun village. Imagine trying to cram all sixteen of us into that tiny two-bedroom bungalow during school holidays.

When the holidays were over and the older ones had to return to their boarding schools or university dormitories, the remaining eight had more breathing space. Seven of us had to sleep in the living room, side by side. Mum and dad had one bedroom, while the grandparents occupied the other. My older brother, Thabiso, had already been moved to the capital to live with our uncle and attend school, while his twin brother, Thabo, had been sent to neighbouring Zimbabwe for boarding school. According to my parents, Thabo was not doing as well as the other students at school. They believed he required serious schooling to progress, and Zimbabwe's education system was one of the greatest in the world at the time. My older sisters, Tebogo and Boitumelo, had already started university in Gaborone, the capital city. Tebogo majored in Public Administration and Political Science, while Boitumelo completed a medical and healthcare degree to become a registered nurse. While watching this, I wished for the day when I could leave home for university and be free.

My mother did what she thought best to support us financially. To supplement my dad's income, she continued her legacy of selling street food in public areas. She chose Maun's crowded bus station to put up her kiosk and offer a variety of vegetables, prepared meals, and beverages. We had to assist her after school while she napped or ran errands. I was always willing to assist during the school days but not on weekends. The weekend was when practically everyone in the village came to town to shop, which meant that all of my classmates would linger and be spoiled by their families. The last thing you want at that age is to be seen selling veggies with other grannies on the side of the road. I felt incredibly embarrassed.

My other siblings weren't as awful as me, and if I saw a classmate approaching our vegetable and fruit stall, I would hide. In desperate times when we locked eyes with one of our schoolmates, we devised a fantastic plan to disguise ourselves. We played dumb, frowned like a clown, and put our tongues out to confuse them.

MICHAEL BANTU-KHOE

And they'll be like, "huh! I thought that guy looked liked Michael, but I guess I was wrong, that's not him". So it worked every time.

When two attractive girls from school arrived to purchase fruits from our kiosk, I bolted. Mum was not available at that time. I swiftly fled and stood behind the counter, claiming to be a customer. Imagine the three of us standing in front of the vegetable booth, chatting to each other and wondering where the vegetable stall owner had gone.

"Maybe they went to the toilet," I said. "Well, too bad for them. Let's go and buy somewhere else," I added.

So, Michael the teenager gambled a few bucks in favour of his school reputation. There were other times when mum was unwell on a Saturday and one of us had to cover her shift, but we made up all kinds of reasons to avoid it. I was always ready to make up a sickness or claim to have chess practice at school, any excuse I could think of.

Dad never offered to assist. Like us, I believe he was embarrassed to be spotted at the fruit and vegetable stand since his co-workers would certainly mock him at work. He merely drove the vehicle loaded with fruits and vegetables and put up the stand. Then he'd go about his business. Dad would come 10 minutes before the mall closed to count the money and carry everything back into the vehicle. That was his regimen, and he followed it religiously.

During the week, sometimes without warning us, Dad would show up at our school with a truck full of fresh fruits and vegetables, chairs and tables, all fastened with a rope. To me, that was an extreme level of embarrassment, and I used to run away from the car when I spotted it miles away. Dad would sometimes stop the fully-loaded pickup truck near the school office parking lot and ask random students if they had seen me. He felt he was helping me by sparing me the 10km trek home. Of course, looking back, I can see my father had good intentions. But back then, I would rather walk 10 kilometres (6.2 miles) each day, Monday through Friday, from our secondary school to our house than be embarrassed by my parents. I am still puzzled to this day that teenage Michael was very comfortable making an arduous and laborious walk through sandy terrain, braving the suffocating heat and at times being subjected to torrential rain and thunder and lightning storms, just so he could fit in and not be subject to ridicule.

Despite my dislike for my mother's business, it paid the bills. It also meant that we always had pocket money to spend during our school lunch periods. Furthermore, part of the proceeds were used to furnish our new home. We moved in after residing with our grandparents for around nine months. I say 'we', but in fact, I'm referring to my dad. Being the eldest child in your family, you were expected to have moved out by then. Otherwise, it sends the wrong message to your younger siblings and, above all, it undermines your parents' parenting abilities.

The house we were supposed to move into was approximately 70% finished, or 'African-ready.' However, the internal water system was not working, so we had to get drinking water from the yard's outside faucet. If it didn't work, we had to go searching for water with large water jugs in the back of our 4x4 pickup truck. When we arrived at a public standpipe, we would sometimes line up for a long time before it was our turn to fill up. When all other possibilities were exhausted, we would risk our lives by fetching water from the Thamalakane River, which flows into the Okavango Delta and is home to a swarm of crocodiles and hippos, so we had to be extra cautious. Once we got the water, we would have to boil it to make it safe for drinking.

Since the home was not yet wired for power, we had to use candles to light our way through the night. It was not an entirely hopeless situation. We spent most of those evenings playing shadow puppets, which was a fantastic way to amuse ourselves and create stories. I also recall the days when I had to complete my schoolwork by candlelight. Those were some of the most difficult days. I also recall doing my schoolwork by candlelight on many occasions. This is not something I believe modern-day students can connect to. I'd be at the mercy of the moonlight sky if we ran out of candles. Our roof, on the other hand, was not your normal roof. There were parts with no roof at all, and you could actually look up and see through to the sky before falling asleep, counting the stars.

MICHAEL BANTU-KHOE

Because they had utilised rusted corrugated iron that they had picked up from the roadside and dumping areas, the roof on the other side of the house was leaking badly. My parents eventually took out a loan to pay for a tile roof, which, by the standards of the village, was considered to be pretty prestigious. People were quick to form opinions about your family's financial situation based just on the kind of roof you had. The following is the order in which social standing was determined: having a tiled roof indicated that you were at the very top of the social ladder, and having a corrugated iron roof indicated that you were from a family that belonged to the middle class. A roof made of grass was a glaring sign of extreme poverty.

In terms of food, it was each man for himself. No, that's not true; I'm just kidding! We were just scraping by and taking each day as it came. There were days when we had enough food and could eat three meals, and then there were days when we could only afford one meal. Chicken and rice was a wealthy man's dish, and I only ate it on rare occasions like Christmas and New Year's Eve. We ate mopane worms or caterpillars when food was scarce during the drought. This modern-day caterpillar frenzy has long been a staple of impoverished people's diets in rural Southern Africa, where it serves as a protein source. They are the offspring of the emperor moth and derive their name from the mopane tree on which they feed. Women harvest caterpillars between April and December, gut them, boil them, and sun-dry them. Their protein, fat, vitamins, and caloric content are comparable to those of meat and fish. Mum had a chilli recipe that she used to create and serve this traditional meal as a side dish in her restaurant. It became very popular, and as demand grew, we often had to get dressed and miss school to help the women gather this tasty treat.

When you're poor, life isn't as bad as some people think. I had some of the most incredible childhood memories, from playing fun children's games like hide and seek and frolicking in crocodile and hippo-infested rivers. We spent most of our time doing outside activities since we didn't have the luxury of watching TV or entertaining ourselves on our mobile gadgets. In fact, we all looked forward to getting home from school and doing different outdoor activities with our buddies. Our parents rarely had to remind us to go outside to

MICHAEL BANTU-KHOE

play. They would occasionally struggle to gather us as the sun began to set below the horizon because we were too busy having fun and losing track of time.

We were often compelled to use our imaginations by playing with bricks and pretending to drive vehicles. When my cousins came to visit for the weekend, we would go dung beetle hunting and scorpion hunting, putting the insects in a cardboard boxing ring for a live entertainment battle. To be honest, this was just as exciting as watching WWE wrestling. Scorpions and dung beetles are mortal enemies; they don't get along at all. When they cross paths, they battle until one of them dies or taps out and flees. We would chant and give them names like John Cena, Triple H, Booker T, and even Kane and his brother, The Undertaker. It was almost identical to the real thing. To spice things up a bit, we'd race the various insects to see who could come in first. That was as interesting as watching a horse race on television.

When the rich kids at school bragged about playing racing cars and FIFA on their Xbox and PlayStation, we looked at them as if they were the ones missing out. So, to simulate FIFA football, we would play football using soda cap players. Each of us would acquire a collection of various beer bottle caps that represented the team's jersey and then put the name of a football player inside each cap. The plastic ball on the tip of an empty roll-on deodorant would then be squeezed and popped out to be used as a pretend ball. The goalposts were just two tiny sticks placed side by side, with a small rock in the centre to act as a goalkeeper. The rules were quite similar to those of a pool game. We took turns playing, flicking the soda caps with our fingers to hit the ball towards the opposing goalpost. Isn't that creative and innovative? And believe me when I say that this was by far the greatest game I've ever played. We'd be soaked in sweat and dust from head to toe by the time we got home, fearing the wrath of our parents.

My parents couldn't afford to get us a Brick Game Retro system when they first became popular in the early 1990s. So, using my Einstein-like brain and one of my mother's hair products, I created my own console game thanks to the laws of physics. The game was simple: I got a Clere BP Pure Glycerine 200 ml bottle and gently spun it upside down. At the back of the bottle, you'll notice that the teeny-tiny air bubbles trapped inside separate and almost immediately make their way towards the central/main bubble. Your objective is to keep them from merging with the central/main one. You keep rotating the bottle quickly in either a clockwise or anti-clockwise direction to prevent that from happening. The faster you spin, the harder it gets. I spent most of my late nights playing that game. To me, that was as good as playing Pac-Man.

We grew more creative as we got older. We began by creating automobiles out of wires and tyres out of tins of soda or beer cans. An internet search will reveal videos of African children engaging in these activities. Seeing how much fun they are having proves once again that you don't need to be wealthy to have a good time. What's the takeaway here? Take advantage of your situation and make the most of what you have.

The following information is supplementary;

Traditional Games that Botswana children born post-2000 may never get to experience.

MICHAEL BANTU-KHOE

Black Mampatile

This is the Tswana version of hide and seek.

KoiKoi

Refers to skipping rope routines that are accompanied by singing, hand-clapping, and rhythmic chants.

Mhele

Botswana's response to chess. It is based on the Tswana traditional way of life, with the pieces resembling cattle. It is mainly played by boys. It is not for the faint-hearted, as it involves a lot of good-hearted intimidation and insults.

Mantlwane

Mantlwane is playing house. In some instances, it was so serious that the children had mini houses carved out of clay. Children would often sneak actual food out of their house and pretend to cook it for the 'family'.

Suna Baby

Suna Baby is a team sport very similar to dodge ball. The balls were usually made out of old plastic carrier bags or old stockings.

MICHAEL BANTU-KHOE

Skonti Bolo/Sewerewere

This is hide and seek with a twist — one player has to look for their playmates, who have to go off and hide. The one player has to find the rest while guarding the ball. The other players can then come out of hiding and kick the ball out of its designated spot. At that point, the ball keeper has to resume the search for the rest of the players. The game can go on for the whole day.

Diketo

This was popularly played by girls. Pebbles are collected and put in a hole. The idea is to juggle throwing one pebble up while distributing a number of pebbles to a dozen or so holes on the ground. Sometimes the players used marbles instead of pebbles. This game was played while sitting down in a comfortable position, directly on the ground.

Molao Molao

This involved an agreement between two people. Whenever one would call out the other's name, they would respond, "Molao!". If the one being called forgot to shout "Molao!", their friend would then be afforded the temporary right to bark orders at him. This ranged from something as cheeky but innocuous as "bring me some water" to the not-so-nice "give me your food for the whole day." How far it could go totally depends on each child's imagination.

Ke Dutse

This literally translates to 'I am seated'. The players agree to announce "I am sitting" each time they take a seat. Failure to do this would result in a slap across the face, usually from behind when least expected. Definitely not something that many parents, least of all the PC brigade of today, would find amusing. But it was fun and was done in that spirit, not at all in a malicious way.

The games vary by name and rules depending on various parts of the country. There are many other games that we have left out that, if not preserved, will be lost forever. And I believe this isn't a problem affecting only Botswana. I have reason to believe that such a problem exists in the western world. As a matter of fact, the words uttered by David Hardy, who is the head of marketing at the National Botanic Garden of

Wales, prove my point. He said, "Nowadays, children have much more to keep them amused – computers, a host of TV channels, and smartphones – something older generations didn't have.

As a result, youngsters miss out on getting dirty in the mud and puddles or simply spending time in the fresh air. "These traditional activities can be a great way of encouraging children to spend more time outdoors, get more exercise, and create more memories than they will get from simply sitting in front of a computer or TV screen.

MICHAEL BANTU-KHOE

A POOR START

RICH ENDING

MICHAEL BANTU-KHOE

This chapter will take you on a journey through the years in our newly completed house. I'll start with what I like to call "the race to the bathroom" to show you what happens on a regular Monday morning before everyone goes to school. My older sister Keabetswe or my younger brother Khumo would wake up at 5:00 a.m. and start boiling water for a bath. We didn't have any indoor hot water, so we had to combine hot and cold water in a bucket. We would boil the water on the gas stove, but when the gas ran out, we had to go outside and build a fire with wood. I didn't like it, particularly during the colder months or after a heavy rainstorm, since it was difficult to start a fire, especially with damp firewood. We would have no choice but to bathe in cold water and remain shivering for the rest of the morning. Alternatively, we were compelled to implement Plan C: no washing at all. Plan C seemed easier and more enticing during the harsh winter, but it was riskier.

At school, the teachers, along with the prefects would undertake random hygiene and cleanliness inspections. Then, immediately after the school assembly, we were all required to line up outside in a straight line for a hygiene check before entering our classrooms. There would be two lines: one for boys and one for girls. The girls would be inspected by a female prefect, while the boys would be checked by male prefects. It was like being checked-in at the airport and passing through the X-ray machine before being permitted into the waiting room. It was terrifying because 99% of the time, I was afraid of being exposed in front of the crowd. Even though I knew I took a bath, I would be frightened since anything may happen. You'd receive a good hiding if you were discovered with unbrushed teeth or stinky armpits, unpolished shoes, uncombed hair, or even dry skin. That was the way things were back then. But I am afraid corporal punishment in schools was and still is a method of discipline for the majority of African children.

On the other hand, having dry skin was a sign among black children that they did not shower. Even if you thought you could get away with applying Vaseline or any other moisturiser to your face, they would still inspect your calves, and that was always a dead giveaway. In severe instances, you may be sent home to bring your parents to the principal's office. It was a frightening and humiliating experience to be sent back home because you had not showered or bathed. People would gossip about you and make fun of you behind your back, and from that moment forward, you would be bullied in this manner.

My fears were warranted. I had to be extremely careful and disciplined to avoid these instances. It was expected that regional water and electricity blackouts, commonly known as load shedding, would occur. This meant we had to find another means to get ready and to school on time. We would sometimes have power and water outages at the same time, necessitating the use of a backup generator. Some wealthy households in our area had large conservatory tanks. We had empty huge oil barrels that had been cleaned on the inside, which we would fill with water the day before. This was the most cost-effective method of storing vast amounts of water.

Because there was no power, we had no choice but to depend primarily on the fire that we had built outdoors for heat and comfort. That entailed gathering firewood from the farm and stockpiling it in our shed days prior. The water that we boiled over the fire in the backyard was used to make coffee for breakfast, and we also bathed using part of the water that we boiled. We couldn't iron in the house because there was no power, so my parents devised another wonderful solution. They bought us an old charcoal iron, known as aene ya magala in Setswana. The charcoal iron was cumbersome, had an antiquated appearance, and was known for leaving scorch burns on our school uniforms.

MICHAEL BANTU-KHOE

Antique Charcoal Iron

The process of ironing would go as follows: first, you would remove coal from the fire, and then you would place it inside the iron. Then, after the iron had reached the desired temperature, you would proceed to iron your garments while maintaining control of the temperature by placing a damp cloth next to the iron. The base of the iron needed to be cooled down with the wet towel about every minute and a half. If you forgot to do this, then whatever you were ironing would likely burn. I learnt this the hard way and had to wait until the next term to buy a new shirt. Meanwhile, I went to school

MICHAEL BANTU-KHOE

wearing the same charred shirt and covered it with my school jumper/sweater.

The chaos that greeted me when I woke up was nothing in comparison to what happened afterwards. Any big family's home will always be chaotic, particularly in the mornings. Fights erupted and hidings were usual; someone's school shoe would go missing, my mother would often shout at me to assist my younger sister with her schoolwork, or sometimes someone spent too long in the bath, resulting in a lengthy line for the bathroom. Simply stated, the mornings were a living hell.

There was never a set schedule for who should take the first shower, when, or for how long. Whoever awoke earliest and heated the water would have the honour of bathing first. Keabetswe, my older sister, would take forever to get dressed in the mornings. She would spend a long time doing cosmetics, and I couldn't comprehend how a human being could spend so much time in front of the bathroom mirror. Our bathroom door lacked a lock for a long time; in fact, the doorknob vanished quickly after someone thought it would make an excellent toy. So it was expected that any of your siblings may come in on you while you were showering, and you would have to cover your modesty and shout at them to leave. We always rushed through breakfast, never ate together at the table, and were always racing against the clock. Every morning, the kids going to school would go through at least two loaves of bread.

Dad insisted that everyone be up and ready to go by seven o'clock in the morning. I mean totally dressed and waiting for him in the truck. If you were delayed for whatever reason, you risked being left behind or experiencing his wrath first-hand. Every morning, my father woke up at 6:45 a.m. to drive us to school. He still does the same thing to my younger siblings to this day. Because of his experience in the military, maintaining such a regimen came much more naturally to him.

The seating arrangement in the truck was quite clear as we drove out for school. Due to the fact that it was a pickup truck with just two doors and an open rear, the smaller children would sit in the front, while the older children would sit in the back. In the winter, it is possible to fit four people in the front seat together with the driver by having the two younger passengers sit on the laps of the two older ones. On several occasions, we were stopped at roadblocks, and the officers would either issue my father a ticket or let him go with a warning. Those of us who had to ride in the back of the pick-up truck had no choice but to brace ourselves for the bitter cold and, on occasion, the pissing rain. If we went out in the dead of winter, we would make sure to have a blanket with us so that we could be warm and cosy.

A few of the vehicles who were behind us found this amusing. They would occasionally blow the horn and laugh at us as they drove passed us because the wind blew the blanket off our feet while we were holding the top of the blanket tightly to keep it from flying off. My dad, though, was never bothered. I mean, he would peek in the rear-view mirror sometimes to check on us, but his main concern was making sure that the youngest child arrived on time for school so that the headmaster would not give her a hiding or a good thrashing for being late. The rest of us, he didn't care about it so much. He would frequently joke: "Lona ba batona akere le siame, le senka thupa." Which translates, "You older ones can endure a hiding. Besides, I think you need one."

Like most African parents, education was everything to them. My mum and dad instilled in us from the outset the importance of education and the desire to pass and achieve. As a result, the majority of my siblings fared well in school. Despite the fact that we all did well in school, I was the odd one out since I was the least talented of them all when it came to sporty activities and games. To put it another way, I am the only kid in my family who does not have a certificate of achievement. I'm afraid there is no awards or prizes. My older twin brothers filled our living room from floor to ceiling with karate trophies and medals from local and international tournaments. The rest of my other siblings got similar trophies for table tennis, badminton, sprinting, math and science, high jump, softball, football, beauty pageants, and a variety of other activities in which I was not talented.

But the one edge I had over them was the early investment my parents made in my schooling. I was the only one of twelve children who was sent to an English nursery or preschool between the ages of four and five, which was a big deal at the time. That, I suppose, is why my accent differs so much from the rest of my siblings. My parents must have had some spare income since the school fees were not cheap. You began standard one or grade one at primary school when you were six or seven years old. Unlike other children, I did not cry when I was left off at preschool, according to Mum. Instead, she said that I seemed optimistic and eager.

Being left off at school became a dreaded ritual as I grew older and entered high school. Like many teens, I was highly self-conscious and worried about how others saw me, particularly my classmates. My father's car was nice, but it was also rather antediluvian. It was a 4x4 Mazda pick-up truck, a strong Japanese vehicle. However, the one we had was a little rusted. Its time was running out. There were times when it would break down or run out of gas, and we would abandon it and walk wherever we needed to go. It was also awkward to have to push it while Dad or Mum attempted to start it. I received a lot of flack at school for being late because our car wouldn't start. That excuse worked the first time, but when you repeat the same thing over and over, the teacher concludes that you're making it up. As a result, the whooping began. I recall pestering my parents about selling that old junk to purchase a brand-new car, but they always laughed at me. Finally, mum would say, "work hard so you can buy it for us."

Dad grew fond of the old Mazda, and he was content with it since it was useful on the farm. I recall hating the fact that we weren't rich like other families and drove a clunker. I was so embarrassed to be spotted by my classmates that I used to request that my father drop me down five minutes away from the school gate so that I could walk from there. My excuse was that the school's little back gate was closer to my classroom, thus travelling all the way around to the front entrance would be pointless. I still believe he bought that narrative.

Aside from the wet dream incident, secondary school was OK for me. It influenced my outlook as a teenager, and it is where I met my first girlfriend, had my first fight, excelled at chess, and participated in national chess competitions.

Among the memories stated above, the one I'm least proud of is my first genuine fight. Remember that my elder twin brothers are also professional gold medallists in karate. So you'd think I'd be lethal in combat merely by osmosis, right? Wrong! My "fight" lasted less than a second. I have no idea what we were fighting over, but I do remember both of us getting our heckles up, only for my opponent to sneak up on me and smash his right knee into my balls. I fell into his arms, as though giving him a bear hug. I'd never experienced such agony. I used to believe that I would never be able to have children. That was my first and only school fight. I knew I had to avoid any possible clashes from then on. I'd be better off focused on becoming a geek and excelling in school.

Being exposed to the realm of chess had several benefits. As a natural deep thinker, I appreciated the chance to tackle an issue while thinking three or five steps ahead. However, it is the anticipation of your opponent's chess piece movements that motivates me the most. It is addictive, akin to mental candy. Losing a chess game felt extremely personal, whereas winning or drawing against some of the top elite players earned you a lot of reputation and respect in the geek world.

It's still one of my phone's most addictive games. And speaking of phones, I come from an age when mobile devices were not permitted on school grounds. So, with the first girl I dated, we spent a lot of time – literally – face to face. Her name was K.Lo, much like J.Lo, but better. She was a ballroom dancer and aspiring top fashion model who won the school beauty contest. Above all, K.Lo was the daughter of a priest in our church. In fact, she and I became friends because both of our mothers sang in the same church choir. I had a huge crush on K.Lo. I recall the first time we met while attending one of the church services on Sunday, and I've been waiting for the right moment to ask her out.
I waited so long to ask her out since she was infamous at school for turning down boys who weren't precisely her type. You had to be first and foremost attractive, a frequent churchgoer, and, most importantly, make her laugh and smile, and you'd have opened the key to her heart." Those were the comments made by one of

K.Lo's closest friends, who confided in me. I took what she said to heart, and eventually worked up the courage to ask her out on a date since I thought like I was in a position of strength.

I remember, as a pick-up line, telling a biblical joke that even a preacher's daughter thought was funny. The punch line went on like this; Once upon a time, a young Christian couple had just started dating and got along beautifully. So, one night, when he thought his date was bored, he attempted to impress her by inserting some bible verses into their text message conversation just for fun and to show off how reeeeally pious he was— because who doesn't like being too religious? Well, it turns out that this simple act summoned an army of Angels from Heaven's Gate to come crashing down on him!

While they continued to text each other back and forth and back and forth. He intended to send his girlfriend a verse from 1 John 4:18 that states, "There is no fear in love, but perfect love casts fear out, because fear restrains us." "Indeed, the one who is fearful has not been made perfect in love". However, as he was composing the message, he failed to include that the scripture to ponder was "1 John 4:18." Instead, he just typed "John 4:18" and pressed the send button. Following the receipt of the SMS, the girlfriend opened her bible to the passage "John 4:18" and aloud recited the following words: "For you have had five husbands, and the man you now have is not your husband." This you have said truthfully." Hahaha! Can you imagine her expression when she read it for herself in her Bible? K.Lo almost fell out of her chair laughing so hard at the joke. That was the start of our friendship. We began dating and quickly became close friends, nearly inseparable.

I recall her attempting to get me to be her ballroom dancing partner. I refused, only to realise that if I didn't dance with her, another man would gladly fill my shoes. In all honesty, I looked ridiculous in those slick salsa dancing pants or even worse, doing cha-cha-cha dance moves with two left feet. I felt more confident playing chess. Today, when I watch shows like Strictly Come Dancing, I say to myself, "Those guys wouldn't have a chance against K.Lo and me."

MICHAEL BANTU-KHOE

When I was in high school, I discovered that I preferred listening to hip-hop music than any other kind of music. The decade of the 2000s was a golden era for young and upcoming musicians and artists. We used to have CD collections and Walkman with cassette tape recordings of our favourite musicians and bands. Some of us who dared to rap carried a "Song Lyric Book" in which we scrawled ideas and logos and put down our hot lyrics. Then we'd show off our skills in the streets by freestyling to any beatbox or rhythm, competing in rap battles, forming bands, and entering talent shows.

My cousin and I were the co-founders of many bands, and one of them was named The Master-bation Crew — Where You Come First (that was our cheeky tagline). Just a bunch of guys that not only took pleasure in their art but also, like Prince, spoke about being the master of one's own destiny and owning your masters or music publishing. You'll be disappointed to learn that the band never took off. We both parted ways due to disagreements, and I formed with my mates a four-man band called The 4-Skins. Likewise, it never got off the ground.

MICHAEL BANTU-KHOE

We held daily hip-hop school public debates over who the greatest rapper was, who won the beef between Jay-Z and Nas, 50 Cent versus Ja Rule, and so on and so forth. These debates took place when we were hanging out in our school gardens and on our basketball courts. The passionate debate about who, between Tupac Shakur and the Notorious B.I.G, is more deserving of the title of "The Quintessential Rapper" was one of the events that stood out to me the most. It felt like an unscripted episode of Dead-End Hip Hop or the Complex Show back then with DJ Akademiks and Joe Budden.

I'm surprised that the young men who were often extremely outspoken at these gatherings and kept the debates lively and entertaining didn't go on to pursue careers in this industry. The vibe among these friends of mine was incredible. Bear in mind that virtually all of us lacked access to the internet at the time, thus the majority of our knowledge came from reading hip-hop publications such as The Source and XXL magazine, listening to Hip Hop Radio talk shows, and TV shows like MTV and VH1. We would couple this with our personal take on the subject. As a youngster who was about to become an overnight rap phenomenon, it was about this time, that I felt an electrifying sensation and developed a musical ear.

At the age of 18, just before I was about to go to university, I became aware of a part of me that I had never previously considered to be there. I broke the record for the youngest rapper in the history of Botswana's hip hop scene when I produced a popular hip hop song. It happened overnight, and no amount of planning or anticipation could have prepared anybody for it. This is all thanks to two geniuses who have supported me from the very beginning. It is a huge blessing in my life that they saw my potential at a young age and helped me develop it. These two individuals are B.K. Proctor and my older brother, Thabiso, a.k.a. Shawn Dee. They have now become industry moguls and continue to shape and inspire new and rising talent.

I had finished my GCSEs and had requested to live with Thabiso, who was working in the city and had rented a one-bedroom apartment at the time. At that point in time, he worked as a freelance journalist and aspired to become a filmmaker. He needed an additional hand on one of his projects and invited me to help him. He was working as a film director on a local hip-hop documentary. While Thabiso was busy managing the cameras, I was in charge of setting up the lights for the scene and holding the boom microphone.

After what seemed to be a long day of work, my brother went to BK and said,
"Yo, BK, did you know that my little brother is a talented rapper?
" I was like, "Huh?"
"Yeah, the young man can rap and does it well," he proceeded on. "He's got some rhymes under his sleeve." At this point, I made a concerted effort not to back down, but to my astonishment, the producer turned to me and asked,
"Are you sure you want to do this?" "I want to hear what you have to say."
Enter the recording studio, put on some headphones; I will play you some instrumentals, and from there it is completely up to you what you want to do. Don't worry, "he added, "we can always erase it if we don't like it." I decided to just go for it. When he started playing the

beat, I started bobbing my head like Jay-Z did in an attempt to figure out the rhythm. I had hardly finished my sentence when I informed him that we could begin. I then proceeded to do a freestyle, and while I was rhyming and spitting my groovy lines, I could tell that they were quite pleased. Their expressions changed drastically, as if they had just unearthed a priceless gem from the muck. To make a long tale short, one of the songs that we wrote and recorded that night went on to become the most popular song in Botswana for two years running. In point of fact, it was played on the radio so often that it evolved into a party song.

Surprisingly, I wasn't a fan of it at first, but after performing it several times, I began to enjoy it. So it really started my career as a musician, and very soon after that, I began travelling the nation, playing at music festivals and places ranging from nightclubs to concert halls. I began conducting TV and radio interviews, as well as appearing in periodicals. My life had entirely transformed. I was enjoying a luxury lifestyle at the pinnacle of my prosperity. Fame and money were everything to an 18-year-old. I wanted to keep it for the rest of my life since it meant that my family would be financially secure, and they were overjoyed.

———————————

SAYONARA I'M

OFF TO

UNIVERSITY

MICHAEL BANTU-KHOE

The day, which I had been eagerly anticipating for a very long time, finally came. I couldn't wait any longer to "gerara here," and for the very first time, I was going to have my very own private bedroom and bed; eat whatever I wanted; stay up as late as I wanted; and basically live by my own rules. I was on the verge of becoming an independent person and flying solo. I had achieved a perfect score in all of my GCSE exams, and as a result, I was offered an academic scholarship to study abroad. I could choose any degree I wanted, but my parents had already decided which one I would pursue. It was already set in stone. I enrolled in a degree programme in architecture. One of the top institutions for the course was the Limkokwing University of Technology in Malaysia. Around two hundred other students had received the same scholarship and had all selected the same institution.

I wasn't the first member of my family to go overseas. My older brother, Thabiso, had spent four years in Melbourne, Australia, studying film and television at Swinburne University. So he was the ideal person to inform me about living as an international student. It is important to note that at this point in my life, I had never flown on a plane before, had never used an ATM, and had no clue what a passport was. Thabiso was the one who showed me how to swipe my bank card for purchases and how to place your card into the ATM while vigilantly glancing around to ensure no one was peering over your shoulder as you punched in your PIN.

Believe me, I was very attentive to his lessons, and he didn't have to tell me twice. I was good to go.

Finally, I had to say good-bye to my parents and the rest of the gang. It was a bit of an emotional exchange. Even though I wanted out, I couldn't fathom my life without them. I was not expecting a hug from my dad, but he surprised me. Then, out of nowhere, things started to go weird. He thought that now would be the most appropriate time to have the "sex talk" with me. Remember, we have never had a one-on-one father-son open discussion, particularly concerning sensitive topics like this. My only previous exposure to sex education came from my biology classes. To say the least, it was embarrassing, but I understood what he was trying to convey.

My father addressed me with a solemn expression on his face and cautioned me, saying, "Son, don't go out there and start having kids. Neither your mother nor I will be raising any grandbabies. Do you hear me?" "Yes, sir," I gently answered. "And I can assure you that you will not hear from me about any kids." All I'll be concerned about is my education and getting good grades, that's it."

MICHAEL BANTU-KHOE

LIES! In the end, I did have a child, but it was 12 years later. Nonetheless, I was determined to keep my word and I didn't want to let my father down. The following day, I had to get myself organised and geared up for a trip to Malaysia that would last for 21 hours. I travelled from Gaborone's Sir Seretse Khama Airport to Johannesburg, then to Dubai, and finally to Kuala Lumpur, Malaysia, through Singapore. My itinerary piqued my interest. I was prepared to face the world for a guy who grew up in the hamlet. From watching my passport get stamped for the first time to going back and forth on an escalator and moving walkways, I felt like a child in a candy store. I was awestruck by all of the beauty that I was surrounded by at the time we arrived at Changi Airport in Singapore. The experience of seeing the world's highest indoor airport waterfall gave me chills, and I realised that whatever was ahead in my life was going to be worth it.

In Malaysia, I was able to make new friends. We would socialise together by going to parties, drinking, and attending more parties. Disclaimer: in order to protect both the innocent and the guilty, some of the identities have been altered. In spite of this, some of the schoolmates I befriended were Babatunde, Big Sam-Sam, Tumelo, Frank, Moses (a.k.a. Mouza) and Skinny Dave. All seven of us were able to get along so well. In addition to that, Frank too was a rapper, he would accompany me to some of my gigs, and together we were like Batman and Robin. As a result of our performances at nightclubs and school functions/events, we gained a strong following at our university campus.

Despite this, Sam and I clicked and struck up a close friendship because we were from the same village. Big Sam was like an older brother to me. He had only been in Malaysia for a week when we arrived, but in that short length of time, he had already discovered all of the best hangouts and spots where one can let loose and have a good time. When we arrived, he had already become something of a tour guide for us.

My university was quite diverse in its student body and faculty. On paper, it seemed to be quite welcoming and comprehensive in scope. Limkokwing University was heralded for its advancement in technology and cultural diversity. Because of the remarkable success it had in

Botswana, the institution decided to establish a second sizable campus in Gaborone, the capital city of Botswana. During orientation, many Batswana found the university pamphlets and welcome videos to be interesting and informative. The underlining message was that somehow, no matter where you were from, you would be welcomed and accommodated in Malaysia. Although this was partly true, the reality was a bit different.

At first, even among the Africans, we had our own little social groups. During that time, we restricted our social interactions to those of our own country. Even within this group, the people who shared your background were the ones you considered to be your closest friends. My biggest connection in our loft was with Big Sam-Sam since he, like me, was originally from Maun. Babatunde and Mouza were both from the same village, and Tumelo and Skinny Dave were home buddies. As for the others, well, if their homeboys were not available, they gravitated towards the nearest ethnic group, and that is how Frank got stuck with us.

LIFE IN AN AIR-CONDITIONED HELL

I always likened walking into the university cafeteria to arriving at a United Nations summit. Just as each country's delegate is assigned a specific seat at a table marked with the name of their country, the students at the school cafeteria were often segregated according to race and ethnicity.

The Asians would congregate on one side of the cafeteria, the Nigerians on another side and a few other Africans in another part of the cafeteria. But, over time, we began to mingle. We would learn a few things about them, and they would learn a few things about us. For example, they knew that most Africans were always late for lectures, and when it came to submitting our assignments, we would wait until the very last minute.. Procrastination was our game plan. Also, black people always sat at the back of the classroom; that's just how we rolled.

I picked up a lot from people of Asian background. They performed a far better job of working together as a cohesive unit, and they gave education a much higher priority than we did. They immersed themselves in whatever they were studying. Even when they were engaged in combat, they fought as a unit. Working as a team is not one of our strengths as Batswana. Despite coming from the same place, we still look out for our personal interests ahead of others. I did that as well, and my friends were the same. We were genuine friends, yet at the same time, we competed against one another.

In my culture, there is a three-word phrase that, when said, conveys a great deal of meaning. "Jealous ya Motswana," which translates to "We would rather see our fellow man fail than prosper/triumph without us." This mindset has influenced our country in little ways, and it can be seen in our way of life today. A few years later, I recall hearing some Batswana businesspeople declare, "I would rather pay a white person than deal with a Motswana," and that statement has stuck with me ever since. You would think that it only means that Batswana are bad people to conduct business with.

However, as a Motswana, you quickly get the underlying meaning. It is hardwired within us to desire to excel on our own and stand out from the pack. So just by observing others, I learned a lot from them. Nigerians were like big brothers we both admired and despised. We appreciated them when they stood up for us when we faced bigotry or discrimination. For most Batswana, we are too easy going for such things. We despised the Nigerians when they tricked us in business and dated our girlfriends. They used to boast about dating our attractive girls because of their gigantic butts. Furthermore, the majority of Nigerians we met in Malaysia were wealthy, so our girls were instantly drawn to their lifestyle. What's more, I lost one of my ex-girlfriends to a Nigerian.

Despite this, I appreciated their hustle. Nigerians did not sit and wait for chances; instead, they created opportunities for themselves. Malaysia had a large number of Nigerians, who started to occupy and monopolise several enterprises. Nigerians, for example, ran nightclubs, entertainment venues, and African churches. They were the lords of the nightlife, hosting celebrities from all over the globe and organising music performances and festivals. As a result, they swiftly became wealthy and well-known. My friends and I attempted to emulate their hustle by organising music festivals and smaller-scale events. However, since the Nigerians were in charge, we had to go through them to accomplish our mission.

That's how stupid we were. Assume a wealthy Malaysian tycoon owns a famous nightclub. Instead of us dealing with him directly, a Nigerian hustler/con artist would outwit us or get there first and beat us to the punch, preventing us from having to deal with the real boss directly. In truth, the Nigerian would be acting and speaking to us as if he were the club's owner and CEO. As a result, we would unintentionally strike deals with him. He already knew the owner's per-night pricing plan and charged us his intended amount to get the lion's share of the profit. We fell for the bait, but, if I'm being really honest, our efforts were futile.

After a string of concerts, regardless of how many events we hosted that were completely sold out, we always just about broke even. We began blaming and getting into fights with one another, and we ultimately decided to discontinue conducting business together. Ruben attempted to host his own shows, but he was unsuccessful. His side-hustle business failed, and he found himself in a deep financial hole as a result. In a nutshell, the Nigerians ate him alive and forced him out of business. It was only then that I realised I couldn't lead two separate lives at the same time. It had only been a few months since I started university, and my grades were suffering as a result of focusing so much of my attention and energy on the music industry. I really wanted to be successful in both areas so that I could make my parents happy. Instead, I felt like a failure and that I had let everyone down. When I started to show signs of severe depression, I numbed my feelings and emotions by taking drugs and drinking too much. It came to a point where I had to choose school over music because it impacted my mental health. Some of my family, friends, and admirers were not pleased with my choice. In retrospect, I did the equivalent of what Dave Chappelle did at the height of his career. He walked away, leaving everything behind and didn't give anyone a plausible explanation.

If I hadn't taken that decision, I very certainly would have failed all of the courses I was taking in that first semester, and I would have been on the next flight back to my home country. That was, sadly, the final outcome that awaited each individual student from Botswana under government sponsorship who failed most of their modules. If you are unable to maintain the required level of academic achievement, you will be kicked out of the university and, at the same time, have your scholarships revoked or terminated. Other African students who were obviously self-sponsored used to be envious of us Batswana students. They believed that those who disregarded their studies and subsequently lost their scholarship had squandered a once-in-a-lifetime opportunity, and this at times infuriated them. Only now do I understand why.

See, to tell the truth, when measured against other countries in Africa, the people of Botswana have it quite easy. According to the Kimberley Process Certification Scheme, our country has become the second-largest producer of conflict-free diamonds. Most of Botswana's prosperity is directly attributed to the diamond sector. Even the centrepiece of Meghan Markle's engagement ring, which weighs six carats, is a Botswana-sourced diamond.

To put this into perspective, Botswana is the only African nation where individuals are paid to attend university or college. Students at universities and colleges are given a monthly stipend, which varies based on where they live. For example, if you attend a university in Botswana, you would earn somewhat more than £100 per month, which is plenty if you live at home and do not pay rent. Furthermore, exceptional performers like myself were sent abroad or funded by the government to study in the United Kingdom, America, Canada, Cuba, Malaysia, and Russia. You just pick where you want to go based on your grades.

Obtaining government sponsorship entitled one to specific advantages or benefits. Each and every month, we received significant quantities of money. We received around £500 per month when I was in Malaysia, plus an additional £500 for our book allowance. That was top money when converted to Malaysian currency. We were making far more than local politicians and even most of our lecturers and professors at the time. As a consequence, burglars and cab robbers/thieves targeted us. It also meant we could buy our way out of trouble. For example, If the police detained us, for instance, we could simply bribe our way out since we had the money. The negative impact of this was that it led to us developing a very reckless and materialistic attitude.

In class, I recall making fun of a Motswana student for wearing the same shoes and refusing to spend his money on new clothes. The whole class taunted and tormented him over it, which I instigated. I subsequently discovered that he was accumulating money to construct apartments for his family back home. He is now sitting comfortably, enjoying the benefits of his thriftiness. I wish I had learned financial literacy at that age. Most Batswana students partied and drank heavily. Unfortunately, one or more Batswana passed away every month as a result of excessive drinking or other complications connected to it. People would fall from ten-storey buildings because of this.

I remember one traumatic incidence involving a Motswana man who died after falling from a seven-story building. My friends were at their flat with him at the time. He had come to them in an inebriated state while they were busy working on their school projects and assignments. They were insistent that he remain and sleep over, but he categorically declined their offer.

MICHAEL BANTU-KHOE

A few minutes after he left their apartment, the guys got a call from the security officer, asking whether they knew such and such, to which they answered, "Yes!" The security guard then said flatly, "Your friend is below... he fell from the building." Everyone was in shock. We wanted to check whether it was true since the ambulance and emergency services did not react soon enough. His corpse laid there lifeless and shattered, with blood splattered all over the place. He was there for hours before the forensic team arrived. This horrifying image was observed by a large number of people in the student apartments. You could see his remains merely by looking through the passageways or through your back windows. We were all deeply saddened, and our hearts, thoughts and prayers went out to his family in Botswana. We didn't know for sure what actually happened, whether he committed suicide, or that he had been pushed, or had been the victim of some kind of witchcraft. The truth is we will never know. Of course, we suspected the latter because of the numerous accounts we had heard from the local people. Witchcraft is practised in Malaysia, and since the practises were equally prevalent in Botswana, it was simple to reach that conclusion.

MICHAEL BANTU-KHOE

Following the tragedy, the Botswana government and authorities quickly intervened to aid the traumatised Batswana students who were onsite. They brought in a Setswana speaking therapist to see how we were doing. They organised many consultation groups and provided one-on-one talk therapy to aid our recovery. This was the very first time in my life that I had ever participated in therapy counselling. I feel that I was psychologically traumatised, and I probably still am. The repercussions of this occurrence started having a detrimental influence on our academic performance and outcomes. As a result, many of the students who were adversely impacted by the tragedy were offered the choice of taking a semester off or transferring to the same institution located in Botswana.

I was on the verge of accepting the second offer, but since I did not want to appear vulnerable in front of my family, I decided to continue living here in Malaysia instead. No doubt, my parents and family knew what was happening, and they were very much concerned, but they turned to the only one thing they felt would help: prayer. My sisters have told me that my mother would send them texts every day at midnight instructing them to get out of bed, get down on their knees, and pray for me while I was in Malaysia. So let's just say their prayers on my behalf became even more intense.

When I was younger, I did not have the same level of spirituality that I have now. One night following that terrible and tragic incident, my friends and I were all chilling together on the couch, watching television. Then, all of a sudden, the cup on the coffee table in front of us suddenly began to move from one end to the other. There was complete silence among us, as if we had just come face-to-face with a ghost. A few seconds later, we immediately sprang from our sofas and ran into our own bedrooms as quickly as possible. After all, this is the kind of stuff that happens only in movies. We waited and waited and waited some more, before anything happened. Finally, Moses entered our room with a Bible and a cross, as if to drive away the so-called bad evil spirits.

It may seem foolish today, but we were just kids, and we were responding in the only way we knew how. We were afraid to dwell in that flat and began looking for alternate housing the next day. Because I was the most scared or chicken, I opted to stay at my girlfriend's apartment for a few days till we figured it out. Years later, I came to the realisation that the sliding cup may have been a normal occurrence; for instance, when the cup is put on a glass table that is damp or moist. I came up with this hypothesis myself, so I didn't bother alerting my friends about my discoveries. Instead, I'll let them go wild with their imaginations.

LIFE IN AN AIR-CONDITIONED HELL

MICHAEL BANTU-KHOE

THE REASONS

WHY I HATE

PRANKS

MICHAEL BANTU-KHOE

Being popular, having a degree of fame, and living away from home all at once has a significant impact on a young person. I was experiencing first-hand what the dark side of instant success and skyrocketing to new heights looked like. I found that the more I tried to get fame, the less content I got. Being an influencer looked like a good concept in principle, but in practice, it turned out to be less than ideal when you were constantly surrounded by individuals whose only goal was to use, exploit, abuse, and take advantage of you (not exactly flattering).

I was barely eighteen years old, and I felt tremendous pressure to be popular and successful in music. At that point in my life, it seemed like the whole world revolved around me, but what does it truly do for you when everything goes wrong? Because of my celebrity, I was able to be a so-called "player" or "lover boy," dating various beautiful women and having as many girlfriends as I wanted. I even had a girlfriend who invited me into her group, where we smoked pot every day until 2 a.m. in the basement of a mutual friend.

Aside from that, I did what most celebs do: I partied every night, with drugs widely available. The old Michael was toxic and unappealing; I was irresponsible and inconsiderate, always drinking and experimenting with drugs, and often in and out of relationships. My life was a never-ending vicious circle. I was in the wrong crowd and had failed to prioritise my schoolwork, let alone my health and wellbeing, which was becoming more apparent. If you met me back then, you'd have assumed I'd just escaped from a psychiatric hospital. "Hurt people hurt people," as the saying goes. This struck a chord with me at the time.

Because Malaysia is a tourist hotspot and near to Thailand, Vietnam, and Indonesia, it was cheaper to visit these countries for a weekend and relax somewhere to re-energise. Malays are warm and welcoming, as they are charming, which is an added bonus. Learning Bahasa, one of Malaysia's primary languages, was required as part of our school curriculum. In order to do this, it was necessary for us to immerse ourselves in their culture and learn about some of their architectural accomplishments. Malaysia is also a Muslim-majority nation, so as a Christian, I was taught to respect other people's religions.

Surely, it wasn't a lesson imparted to some arrogant Motswana residing in the same building. He groped a hijab-wearing lady in public. What happened to him thereafter was entirely justified. About thirty Muslim men stormed his apartment and battered the crap out of him. Everyone was watching from their windows to see how it would end. As the throng gathered, it seemed like it would end in mob justice.

According to rumours, the guy escaped by leaping from the 5th floor balcony to the 4th floor balcony and then onto the next one until he reached the ground level and ran to the police station to surrender himself. According to reports, he received a substantial fine and had to appear in court multiple times. After about a week, we spotted the same guy hobbling about on crutches, covered in stitches and bandages. Nobody wanted to be seen with him in public after that.

A few days following that one-time occurrence, I came dangerously close to taking my own life. I came so agonisingly close to committing suicide by leaping from the seventh floor of our apartment building. You may be wondering why this was the case. My so-called friends, however, came up with the idea of playing a prank on me, similar to how Ashton Kutcher or Chance The Rapper prank celebrities on the television show Punk'd. So, my friends concocted this ludicrous narrative behind my back. Everyone was involved except me. All of this began when a few of my mates became aware that the cafeteria lady who served us breakfast liked me more than the others. It was clear to me that it was due to the fact that I had impeccable manners. She would always serve me more food than the others; she'd give me an additional piece of bacon, an extra pancake, and occasionally even let me pay later. That's how much they trusted me. My friends, on the other hand, never got the same perks as I did. I was obviously being rewarded for being a good person and a loyal customer, but my strange friends decided to mess up my otherwise pleasant morning routine.

The cafeteria lady claimed to be from Indonesia. It was difficult to tell if she was Christian or Muslim based on her looks. So, when I returned home from school one day, I was shocked to see a large group of my friends assembled in my apartment. As I walked in, I saw their perplexed expressions or bewildered looks, and my first thought was,

"Oh no! Did someone die? "
At that point, one of them approached me and said, "Bro, did you not hear?"

"Hear what?" I asked.

MICHAEL BANTU-KHOE

"Yo!" exclaimed another. "This guy isn't taking it seriously."

If I were you, I'd take the next flight home".

"What do you mean, next home flight?" I responded.

"What on earth actually happened?"

"Did someone die or something?"

"Nah, nah, it's not that," they said.

"It's nothing to do with that."

They all waited for a few seconds, acting as if they were holding back from saying anything further. Finally, one of them broke the stillness by saying,

"Ey, Mike. Look, buddy, it's the downstairs woman.

"What lady?" I asked.

"You know, the one who always serves us breakfast at the cafeteria?" I overheard the other Malay guy telling someone that their husband is going to come for you, dude.

"What the hell are you talking about, the husband coming for me?" "What did I do?"

My voice had a tinge of annoyance to it.

My friend then went on to say,

MICHAEL BANTU-KHOE

"Yoo! Someone apparently told the husband that you were spotted openly flirting with his wife, and now everyone is hunting for you, dude! So, when Dave and I arrived this afternoon, a random person asked us what apartment number Michael lived in. I informed him. I assumed he was going to deliver food. I'm sorry, dude.

As he spoke, another of my friends entered the apartment, panting as if he had just climbed the whole flight of stairs.

"Ey!" he said, catching his breath.

"What the hell is going on, man? When I entered the building, I saw a large number of Malay men in the reception area. Are they going to look for that guy again? "

Another buddy of mine placed his hands on his head and said,

"Oh, man, I hope not! They are surely going to kill that guy. "

While they were arguing with one another, I was in the background trying to piece together what was going on and wondering whether they had specifically come here to see me. While I was pondering that, the villainous genius who posed as my mate got up and stated,

"Mike, I believe they are here for you, bro! You have no choice but to run or hide or do something before you end up like the other guy. "

I almost threw up. I went to the balcony without thinking and grabbed the railings, ready to jump. But, thankfully, I chickened out when I glanced down and realised how far the ground was. I then thought I needed to go someplace and hide. As I returned to the living room, one of the guys held out a phone and exclaimed, "Bro! I believe it's that lady's husband on the line. He phoned and asked to speak to you."
I slowly picked up the phone and said, "Hello," in the faintest voice.

The person on the other end of the line was speaking fast. I was cursing the invention of cell phones at this time. The guys had managed to find a random Malay man and let him in on the prank. I must say, he deserved an Oscar. He started violently cursing at me over the phone in English and Bahasa. I was holding the phone six inches away from my ear to lessen the pain of the conversation. Before hanging up, he said he and the others were coming up to speak to me. I prayed for the ground to open up and swallow me whole. The guys then suggested I hide, while others pretended to contact the police.

I dashed out of our apartment and down the hallways. And still in mid-flight, I peered through the corridors to check whether anybody was coming up the elevators. Indeed, they were. I quickly made my way to the evacuation stairs and got off on the sixth floor. I remember chatting with a neighbourly South African guy named Mandla. I remember him being quite polite to me. His flat was No. 207 on the sixth floor. I bulleted my way into his apartment without even knocking. The poor guy was about to make out with his new girlfriend from school. So yeah, I kind of poured cold water on his plans for a romantic evening. It didn't even occur to me at first to explain why I had come over.
I was a bit fidgety and kept saying to him,

"Look, bro, I need somewhere to hide until the police arrive."

"I'll tell you more about it later, but it's a matter of life and death, bro! Please, you've got to help me out."

I said this as I drew all of his curtains and switched off his lights to stay hidden. Then, finally pointing to his bedroom, I said,

"Bro, I need to lay low for now." If somebody comes in here looking for me, tell them I'm not here. Okay? "

"Oh yah... okay, no worries, man," He said. You are safe here. Do you want me to call the police or something?" he asked,

"Nah, it's okay, my friends already did that." I said, "They should be here any moment. "
The girlfriend was still in the background, pretending to be watching TV, but really, she was as interested as he was in what was going on. So, I hurried into his bedroom, locked myself in, and then crawled under his bed and stayed put. Thirty minutes passed, and nothing happened. Then, an hour passed, and still, nothing happened. Then two hours passed, and all of a sudden, I could hear a faint voice from outside Mandla's bedroom door, saying,
"Ayo! "Mike, you good? "
 I recognised his voice.
"Yeah, yeah! I'm good, thanks. "

And he said, in a whisper, "Alright, man, let me know if you need anything else."

"Alright, thanks, Mandla," I said.

In retrospect, I'm surprised at how chilled out and understanding this guy was.

I was underneath the bed for over three hours, and my phone was constantly buzzing. It was the guys calling, trying to reach me, but I didn't want to answer. After 20 missed calls, I finally answered the next one. The person on the other end of the line kept asking where I was. I remained motionless, listening for any background noise that may have indicated the Malay guys were in my apartment.

Then, all of a sudden, one of the guys in the background did a Malay voice impersonation and muttered something, and I immediately hung up. My heart was thumping like it was about to jump clean off my chest. Within a few minutes, I heard the front door slam. I was frightened. However, after I realised the South African guy's girlfriend was leaving the apartment, I calmed down. My friends seem to have gone looking for me with the intention of coming clean and telling me that it was all a prank. If only they had texted me to let me know. They did, but I never checked any of my phone messages. Fortunately, they ran across Mandla's girlfriend, who point-blank snitched and informed the lads where I was hiding. I was hiding in the apartment when they arrived. They were quite noisy, laughing madly and screaming my name. I could make out what they were saying as they got closer: "Michael, it was a prank..."Yo, Michael. "Come on out, mate, it's a joke!," followed by a roar of laughter.

As soon as I grasped what they were saying, I felt a mixture of relief and anger at the same time. I crept out, or rather emerged cautiously from my dark, hollow hiding spot/grotto. I could hear my wicked friends roaring or cackling out in hysterics as they struggled to catch their breath from the exertion. After a while, I started laughing along with them, despite the obvious embarrassment I was experiencing. This situation reminded me of the humiliation of the zip incident.

After that prank, I realised how gullible and insecure I can be at times. Before you all start judging me, what would you have done had you been in my shoes? Huh?

MICHAEL BANTU-KHOE

Be honest. I mean, of course, I could have been smarter and seen the tell-tale signs, especially when they handed me the phone with the so-called husband on the other end of the line. I could have even asked how he got their number. But when you are in fight-or-flight mode, you are not really thinking straight, are you? It's hard to use your brain and think logically.

In later chapters, I will dive deeper into this behavioural pattern and how it might affect your mental health. Needless to say, my friends still laugh about this prank. They had no idea that I almost killed myself by jumping from that tower block. Let it serve as a lesson to all of you insane people who like pranking others.

NOT ALL
WOUNDS ARE
VISIBLE

MICHAEL BANTU-KHOE

During the whole time I was in Malaysia, I found myself missing my family and friends back in the United States. It didn't help that I would stay up late working on schoolwork and spend less time talking to my family on the phone than I used to. I want to really look into their eyes. I found myself longing for the

MICHAEL BANTU-KHOE

mundane shenanigans, the infectious laughter, and the home-cooked meals that my mother used to make. As a result, I took advantage of the lengthy break between terms at my school and went to Botswana to see my family. About four times a year, on average, I made the trip back home. It was usually easy to find reasonably priced student packages at the local travel firms. I used to really like being in the air. The many movies, the unlimited free food, and the fact that I could boast about flying were all things that really appealed to me about the flight. Being on an aeroplane seemed like a serious upgrade and a luxury to someone like me, who grew up in a hamlet and was used to travelling by donkey, walking barefoot, and in many cases even walking to most locations as the primary mode of transportation.

I flew economy all the time, never first or business class, but to me, the experience of flying in itself felt like I was travelling first class every time. Over time, my love for flying started to diminish. The more I got on a plane, the more traumatic it got. I know I need to find a way to confront my deathly fear of flying. To this day, I still dread boarding a flight and the feeling during take-off where you feel your stomach moving up to your chest. The worst part is when the aeroplane hits turbulence, and you can see the wings flapping as if ready to snap at any given time. Just thinking about it gives me nightmares. Don't get me started with the landing.

As soon as the wheels are engaged, and the aeroplane touches down, I get really tense every time and I genuinely cannot cope with it. Years later, after spending time in therapy, I realised where this sudden fear of flying came from. When I was in my early twenties, I made the mistake of habitually watching those aeroplane crash investigations you see on TV. If you don't want to be plagued by the same fears, I strongly suggest you do not watch those programmes. They do nothing but mental harm. I got into watching these sorts of shows because of the news reports on the missing Malaysia Airlines flight MH370 in 2014. I thought to myself, "I could have easily been a passenger on that flight." So naturally, I was a little nervous about flying again, even with local Botswana airlines.

I still remember how freaked out I would get whenever the plane went through turbulence. I would be wide awake and shaking throughout the journey. I wouldn't even use the flight toilet for that period, no matter how pressed I was. The movies were not as appealing as before, and I had no appetite. I was doomed to have a meltdown. To give you an example of how crazy it can get, I remember sometime in 2015 when I was flying with a friend to London Heathrow from South Africa. I told my friend about my fear of flying, and he thought I was being a bit dramatic.

Before taking off from O.R Tambo airport, the pilot made his usual welcoming remarks, followed by a few announcements, the kind that put me on edge. He first called out a list of people's names and asked them to identify themselves to the flight attendants. Now, I only found out after the flight that the reason for the announcement was because those individuals were vegetarians. The flight attendants just wanted to confirm their seat numbers to make it easier for them to serve food. Because I had binge-watched programmes about plane hijackings, I got really suspicious and anxious and started to overthink the matter.

In my mind, I thought the names called out were suspected terrorists. So I panicked and wanted to get off the plane immediately. I did not cause a scene, thankfully, but I almost did. When they played the safety video, I was as attentive as ever, and I memorised every detail of what they were saying. I identified where the nearest exit points were located, and how to fetch the safety jacket and safely put on the oxygen mask. I listened intently to how to execute the brace position flawlessly should there be an emergency and, most importantly, to turn off all electronic devices or put them in flight mode before take-off.

That, to me, was the most crucial commandment on the plane. I was ready to obey it wholeheartedly, and like Moses in the Bible, I felt the need to make sure everybody obeyed that commandment. So I looked at everyone near me who was using their mobile phones and tablets to see if they would turn them off. I kept asking my friend, "Did you turn your phone off? Did you? What about your tablet? Is it off? Let me see it! Alright, cool…" I was annoying and a bit of a control freak.

MICHAEL BANTU-KHOE

I began mentally ticking all the boxes of what I needed to do to survive in an emergency. It never occurred to me that if the plane suddenly crashed, everybody on board would instantly die. In my head, I thought the reason the death toll for plane crashes was always high was because most people were not good swimmers. So my theory was that if we crashed into the ocean, our survival chances depended on our swimming abilities. This gave me a bit of confidence, even though I have never swum in the sea – Botswana is a country sandwiched between other countries, and we have no beaches. If we were to crash on land, it would probably be like the widely popular TV series Lost. Again, your chance of survival depended on finding basic food, building a shelter and waiting to be rescued. I had it all figured out in my mind.

Since I didn't have an appetite while flying, I saved what food I could, and I wasn't planning to share it either. As an African, I knew hunger and starvation were as closely related to us as a brother or sister. As a village boy, I could survive on less. I know I can live in the wild among all the wild animals; it would be just as easy for me as it is for Bear Grylls. I also know how to make a fire, drink river water, avoid getting sick, build a shelter in a day and sleep comfortably in a tree. If there were ever a virus outbreak, I had a significant chance of living to tell the tale because I once got stung by a poisonous scorpion when I was a kid and survived. So I must therefore be a mutant or something. Just pondering these things gave me a false sense of security that I could somehow survive this whole thing should anything happen. My mind was running wild. But just when I was starting to feel good about myself, the pilot made another announcement:

"Ladies and gentlemen, this again is your pilot speaking. I hope you are comfortable and managed to all find your seats. If you need assistance securing any of your luggage or seat belts, please contact the nearby flight attendant. Our flight today is expected to last about 10hr 30mins, and we will be cruising at an altitude of 35,000 feet. Overall, we are expecting a smooth and easy flight. However, we should expect some slight turbulence as we cross the equator, but all in all, we wish you a pleasant and happy flight. Thank you once again for flying British Airways."

And then he hung up. Now, this is how I processed that information: "Hi guys; we are expecting some turbulence, turbulence, turbulence, turbulence, there will be plenty of turbulence, turbulence. But make sure your seats are fastened because of *the turbulence, turbulence, turbulence, turbulence, turbulence*. Thank you all for flying with British *turbulence, turbulence, turbulence Airways. Turbulence!*

I began praying silently as we took off. I tried hard not to look outside the window. With every turbulent shake, I thought it would be the end. My eyes were glued to the screen. I wasn't watching movies, I was following the flight's real-time tracker and literally doing the countdown to our final destination. During my observations, I noticed that whenever we were crossing or flying over water surfaces like a river, lake or ocean, the turbulence would begin and intensify, so I knew when to assume the brace position. I timed each spell of turbulence, how long it lasted, and how far apart they were. It was as if I was timing a woman's labour pains.

As we approached the equator, right in the middle of Africa, I became tense and held my friend's hand. It was such a terrible experience for me. When we finally got to London, I did not know that aircraft often circle the airport when it is so busy as they have to wait for the runway to clear. I thought the pilot was having trouble landing the plane or maybe having difficulty seeing through the thick grey clouds. Just like when driving a car through the mist, sometimes it can be hard to see ahead when it's all blurry.

Now, you may be wondering why I am relating these so-called phobias. If you haven't picked up on it by now, I can confirm it for you now that, yes! I do suffer from a mental health condition. I have been diagnosed with clinical depression and severe anxiety for many years now. But, of course, I did not know this when I was flying, which is why my mind often led me through such rabbit holes, leaving me overwhelmed and mentally drained. With my dimples, I could be all smiles, happy and confident, but then I would be the polar opposite and nervous the next day.

Through therapy, I began to dissect and take back control of my mind. I have come to learn that a mental illness does not mean you are weak; instead, fighting against it makes you stronger. Before I delve deeper into this subject, I want you to know that I am no doctor, qualified physician or expert in this field. All the talking points I will bring to this book are strictly related to my personal experience and may or may not apply or work for you. I strongly suggest you seek a medical physician for a clinical assessment and treatment if required. One of the eye-opening lessons I've learnt from therapy was understanding how the body works. Our bodies respond to stress, anxiety, worry and fear in almost the same way by activating the 'freeze, fight or flight' system. However, it is also essential to understand that the part of our brain that deals with this, the amygdala, cannot distinguish between real and imagined problems.

For example, let's say you're comfortably sitting somewhere, and suddenly, a lion walks into the room. Your brain quickly identifies the lion as a danger and therefore prepares the body to engage in a 'freeze, fight or flight' mode. A series of hormones, including adrenaline, are then released inside our bodies to make us hyper-alert, focused and energised. This chemical cascade causes an increased heart rate, respiratory rate and perspiration. Therefore, our heart beats faster when we are frightened so that adrenaline can pump through our blood to other parts of the body. As the heartbeat increases, it causes the breathing rate to accelerate as well.

At that point, your pupils dilate to maximise vision on the target or escape routes. The body also diverts most of its energy away from activities such as food digestion. It is no wonder then that in that moment, it's improbable that you'd feel hungry. Can you imagine facing a ferocious lion and thinking to yourself, "Hmmm, I'm a little bit peckish?" All the resources in your body are fully engaged and focused on this impending threat. When you're in that zone, it's hard to think logically or plan for the future. When you're one-on-one with a hungry lion, you can't say to yourself, "I wonder, what I should eat for dinner? Hmmm." But the lion most certainly can! You cannot think of other things because your mind has zeroed in on either eliminating the threat or fleeing it to survive.

So how does our illustration translate to when somebody has a severe panic attack or anxiety attack?

Remember, the brain can't tell the difference between a real and imagined problem. The more you dwell on a perceived problem, the more it becomes almost real and tangible to you. So how does the brain react? It goes on autopilot mode, thus causing the body to respond the same way as when threatened physically by a lion. So, when you are lying in bed worrying about your future mortgage payments, upcoming exam results or whatever keeps you up at night, remember that the longer you dwell on a problem, the more your body reacts as if a lion is standing in front of you.

You certainly lose appetite because all the energy meant to help with food digestion is now diverted to address the perceived danger. You'd also lose sleep because the body is under attack, and you need all your mental resources to be up and running. At that moment, you cannot think of anything other than the problem in front of you. This is because your mind is fixated on the potential danger. Understanding that truth really helped me tremendously. It helped me see why I felt the way I did when I was hypervigilant on that aeroplane. It's no wonder my anxiety is often high, and I end up feeling depressed days later. So today, I try to take each day as it comes and apply some of the techniques I've learned in therapy. Like Drake says in one of his songs, *"...I feel good, Sometimes I don't..." – God's Plan.* And that's part of life.

Another lesson I learnt from cognitive behavioural therapy (CBT), which aided my recovery, was understanding the power of thoughts. Your thoughts impact how you feel, and the emotions you feel can cause you to act or behave in a certain way. Take for example a negative thought like, "I am a failure" or "I am not good enough". If you keep telling yourself that over and over, eventually, you start to feel sad, which then becomes an emotion. What often happens when you're sad? You isolate yourself or become withdrawn, which then becomes the final act of behaviour.

The same thing applies to positive thoughts. When you keep telling yourself, "You can do this" or "You are really worth it", those thoughts eventually trigger the brain to release a chemical called dopamine, often referred to as one of the happy hormones, which makes you feel well and happy. Happiness is an emotion or feeling, and when you feel happy, your actions end up being positive. So, the next time you want to change a behavioural pattern, ask yourself, "What kind of thoughts do I allow myself to think? Are they positive thoughts, or are they negative thoughts?" Believe me; it's all on you!

As for me, writing this book has been nothing but a cathartic experience. I have never been this open, let alone unobstructed enough to talk about my mental health condition. It's been a closely guarded secret that only a handful of people know about, including my doctor. None of my family in Africa knows about my condition because I feared being labelled and stigmatised, as commonly happens to people suffering from mental health. Depression and anxiety are often lumped together and categorised as everyday stress, like something you could just get over the next day.

You have probably seen on television how the public often treats people diagnosed with depression and anxiety. Some of the gruelling pictures are too graphic and painful to watch. Religious communities often chastise and label you as being demonised and needing deliverance. Because of this, I held back from speaking to family and friends about my condition.

Since relocating to the UK, I understand that depression and anxiety aren't taboo subjects in Western countries compared to where I come from. It's widely covered in the media and talked about in public spaces. Although the stigma isn't completely erased, the attempt to normalise the conversation seems to be paying off. I hope we can one day achieve that across The Motherland and spread some positivity around mental health education. I wish to do my part and help raise awareness to fellow Africans on the continent and in the diaspora. I don't have to go it alone; we need a collective voice from fellow Africans to help break the mental health stigma. Despite it being a mammoth task with many hurdles to overcome, we can at least try to teach the new and upcoming generation how to look after their mental health.

I grew up thinking that my grandfather and dad were private and quiet. It could be that they, too, also battled with depression but didn't know what it was, or they may have even diagnosed it as stress or a result of a lack of faith in God. Many people think that the Bible and medical science are like oil and water and don't go hand in hand. However, you would be surprised at how much they have in common. The Bible is not a medical textbook, nor does it regulate every aspect of human behaviour, but it is always spot on when it comments on issues related to science.

For example, read Genesis 38:28 and Colossians 4:14. You will see that God allowed healthcare practitioners like midwives and physicians to operate among his people in Biblical times. There is nothing in the Bible that would indicate that God was displeased with their use of medicinal plants, ointments, prescribed diets and other health treatments. In fact, Jesus acknowledged that "persons in health do not need a physician, but the ailing do". ~ Matthew 9:12

So, for all those people who promote spiritual healing (also known as faith healing) over medical treatment, this piece of advice is meant for you. I genuinely hate seeing people suffer, especially with mental health. It is like you're locked inside your own prison, the prison of your mind. And I, for one, know first-hand what it's like to be misunderstood and taken the wrong way.

The other day, I was having a conversation with one of my siblings. I was very depressed, to be honest. While we talked, they asked me how I was.

Trying to tiptoe around that question, I said to them, "I'm not feeling so good. I'm feeling a bit down today." I didn't dare mention the word "depression." The truth is, I really wanted to open up and tell them so badly, but the words wouldn't leave my mouth. I am glad I didn't because what followed was a long lecture on how negative I am these days and that successful people never think like that. I understood that the advice came from a good place, and they meant well. They were only looking out for their little brother and trying hard to motivate me into action. But despite their good intentions, it made me feel worse. Next time, I know never to show any sign of weakness or, God forbid, confess my depression status to my family. It would be like taking a bath with a plugged-in toaster.

People with depression often don't want to hear solutions when they are having an episode. The best thing you can give someone going through depression is a listening ear. Do not be quick to offer solutions; just listen empathetically. One person described empathy in such beautiful terms: "Empathy is your pain in my heart." Even if you cannot really relate to what they are going through, try hard to be there for them. Ask them, "What can I do for you?" Most of the time, we know what we need to do yet lack the power to do so.

Not so long ago, I watched a BBC TV programme called Mind over Marathon. I recommend that everyone watch it, even if you do not have a mental illness, because just being aware of another person's condition can help you know how to contribute to their wellbeing. The programme highlights how regular exercise can minimise the impact of depression. Your health may slightly improve for the better just by watching this programme. Still, the more significant challenge, as shown in the programme, is being consistent and developing self-discipline.

MICHAEL BANTU-KHOE

LIFE IN AN AIR-CONDITIONED HELL

MICHAEL BANTU-KHOE

FROM THE LATIN WORD "HUMUS"

MICHAEL BANTU-KHOE

CHAPTER 10

The last time I was still in Malaysia. This time, I am permanently back home in Botswana, and it's the middle of spring 2011. Things didn't go as planned. I ended up dropping out of university. I had a mental breakdown and was back to square one, living with my parents again. I felt like I was a huge disappointment,

MICHAEL BANTU-KHOE

especially to my parents. My music career had also derailed, and nobody seemed to like me anymore. I became a thing of the past, and the world quickly moved on without me, making me feel like sh*t. It was as if I were a plastic cup, here today and gone tomorrow. For months, I would stay in my room, lying in bed, doing nothing at all except feeling sorry for myself. My parents tolerated it for a while, but they could only be patient for so long.

Finally, I was forced to go out and look for a job, which wasn't easy at all. When you don't have a university degree, the struggle is real. I looked for whatever I could find and eventually found a minimum-wage job in a local pest control business, but it wasn't the lowest-paid job I've ever had. The lowest was literally less than £0.50/hr, working for my grandfather after he had asked me to dig a hole in the ground for a pit latrine toilet. On an eight-hour shift, that job took me two days to complete; I should have charged him with child labour and forced him to pay me more! So, by comparison, this new job wasn't as bad as the old one. I was thinking quite positively here, actually.

MICHAEL BANTU-KHOE

My job title was somewhat fancy and illustrious, like Pest Specialist, Exterminator, and Operator, but in reality, I was just your typical rat man. Can you imagine? From being a famous rapper to being a lowly rat man! Now that's got to be the epitome of hitting rock bottom. Local businesses and residents would call the office whenever they had a pest infestation, including rats, flies, cockroaches, bats, bees, termites, and snakes. So basically, if anything was a threat to you, that's where I came in!

I wouldn't say I liked the job, but it was the only thing available at the time. People used to look down on me and feel sorry for me. I had hit rock bottom. This time, there was no hiding or pretending to be dumb because during the day, I had to walk from one business to another. Carrying a briefcase full of pesticides and wearing a bright green uniform with pest control on the front and back to advertise our services. Sometimes I would also be asked to do the night shift, and I grew to like them because it meant less interaction with the judging public and I also enjoyed spending time alone. One of the perks of working the night shift was that the company offered free meals. Working nights came with its own challenges, though, as having to pull 12-hour shifts from 6pm to 6am takes a toll on your health. On top of this, you spend most of your days sleeping.

The night shift went like this: I would be dropped off at a specific business location, let's say a local supermarket the size of Tesco. Sometimes I was alone or, if the task was huge, another colleague would join me. As the supermarket store closed at around 7:00 pm, the store manager and security guards would then lock me inside the store with all my special equipment and suit of armour. If you saw me geared up in the suit, you would think, "Man, this guy works for NASA, and he ain't playing." No matter what you do, you do not disrespect the suit. Loads of men died in that suit due to cancer from inhaling the chemical fumes. But that's not the point.

The point is that I got to let these crazy-ass pests know who the real boss was. I went into the back kitchens and did the damage. I spent entire nights spraying chemicals to kill roaches with my mask on, and trust me, there was always a swarm of them coming at me to avenge their brothers and uncles. Like Rambo, I lay down and set booby traps and rat and mouse traps in storage rooms. I felt like the more rats I killed, the more they multiplied. I was fighting an entire colony of rats all by myself. Whenever I needed to take a short break, I would lie down somewhere on the floor and find a magazine to read or listen to a late-night radio show. By the time the shop opened early the following day for the staff, I would make my exit and go straight home. When I got home, I would usually shower first, have breakfast, and go straight to bed.

However, I did this the other way around a few times because I was so exhausted. For their part, my siblings kept doing what they always do best: making me the laughing stock of the family. I remember going back and forth with them, trying to explain that my night shifts weren't similar to the kind of shifts a night watchman does, patrolling on foot and providing overnight security for buildings.

But they continued calling me a night security guard or a watchman, even though I wasn't either of those things in reality. I guess I needed the laughter to help me get through this painful process. We have to laugh to get over the bridge of pain. At times in life, you have to learn to be humble, just like Kendrick Lamar says. If you don't, then one day life will force you to be. I'm sure most celebrities have had moments like these. Maybe not as bad, but still.

I looked in the dictionary for the word "humble," and I was intrigued to learn that this English word is derived from the Latin word humus, which means ground or earth. And this seemed appropriate since we say that a humble person is down to earth. But I can see how this definition could be misinterpreted by someone with a mental illness or who struggles with low self-esteem. They might look at that definition and use it to justify their extremely negative view of themselves. I had fallen victim to that myself and had allowed feelings of unworthiness to define the Michael I was. However, after re-visiting that exact definition, I somehow felt liberated. I realised that there was more to it than I initially thought.

Being a down-to-earth person does not mean you should be subterranean or underground. We have to think something of ourselves; otherwise, we wouldn't care about our personal appearance. We would almost be suicidal if we thought nothing of ourselves. There is always something valuable that each of us possesses. I had to learn that vital life lesson the hard way. So yeah, being a rat guy became a part of my life for a while until I received an unexpected call.

The call was from my big brother, Thabiso. At the time, he was running a very successful media company. Since I left the music industry altogether, we had drifted apart, and for good reason. He invested quite a lot in me as a road manager, and I let him down by throwing away my career. I hadn't told him about the mental health thing either.

Thabiso worked in the city, and I lived with my parents in the village. But he ended up reaching out, and to this day, I am glad he did. I don't know if it was out of pity or if mum and dad had pressed him to — I will never know. But he offered me a full-time job with good pay on the spot. He asked me to come in as a researcher and scriptwriter and help put together programmes for television. I took the offer and quit my pest control job that same day. I packed my bags and boarded the midnight bus to embark on the 12-hour journey to the city, where my exciting new job awaited.

I spent over five years working with my brother, and throughout those years, I gained a wealth of knowledge about how to run a production set. My brother made sure I didn't get comfortable performing only my assigned role, so I volunteered to do even menial tasks. I didn't get any special treatment, and when I did a shitty job, he didn't hold back from giving me a piece of his mind. Working side-by-side with my brother felt like I was an apprentice learning all the tricks of the trade from the best in the game. Fair play to him; he was, and still is, the best in the game. I will now give you an extract from his Wikipedia page that provides a synopsis of his distinguished career:

"Thabiso Maretlwaneng most recently won the African Achievers Award 2015 for 'Excellence in Film and TV in Africa'. This Honorary Award has previously been bestowed on great icons like Archbishop Desmond Tutu and former Malawian president Joyce Banda. This undefeated five-time African karate champion started lifting Botswana's flag high at a tender age.

MICHAEL BANTU-KHOE

My Brother Thabiso AKA Shawn Dee

MICHAEL BANTU-KHOE

However, these days he is best known for his contribution to Botswana's film and television industry. Maretlwaneng was also recently involved in Hollywood's *A United Kingdom*. The film premiered in 2016 and is based on the romance between Seretse Khama and his wife, Ruth Williams.

Thanks to his outstanding performance as a national karate champion, he earned a scholarship to study at the Swinburne University of Technology in Australia. He graduated with a bachelor's degree in film and television. During his time overseas, he excelled in both arenas. He won a silver medal in the under-60 kg men's individual kumite at the Asia-Pacific Karate Championships in Malaysia. As a film student, he produced the acclaimed feature-length documentary film Head Up. It follows the journey of young black refugees settling in Australia and struggling to break into the country's commercial music industry. The controversial documentary earned Maretlwaneng a distinction from his university. He was the first student to graduate in Australia with a feature-length project and a black hip-hop feature documentary. Head Up also won an award at the New York International Film

Festival in 2009. After working on Botswana's first international film, The No. 1 Ladies Detective, Maretlwaneng founded Dee Zone Productions in 2008. The production company, assisted in 2009 by Botswana's Youth Development Fund, now employs 50 young people annually.

Dee Zone Productions has changed the country's television landscape by hosting various new productions on Botswana TV. These include Maretlwaneng's own 52-episode TV drama, Ntwakgolo, which he produced and directed, addressing issues surrounding HIV. He has also made a 26-episode drama, Pelokgale, that tackles gender-based violence. He is also known for Pula Power, a youth lifestyle programme that showcases Botswana's talent across Africa and the famous Good Morning Africa on DSTV.

While working for my brother, he put me on a project that I took a liking to—researching the impact of HIV/AIDS across Botswana. Of all the projects I worked on, this one was more personal than the others for the following reasons: According to the World Health Organisation and UNAIDS, Botswana faces one of the world's most severe HIV epidemics. At the end of 2019, an estimated 380,000 adults and children lived with HIV/AIDS in Botswana, with an adult prevalence of around 20.7% between ages 15–49. At 20.3%, Botswana has the fourth-highest HIV prevalence globally after South Africa, Lesotho, and Swaziland.

Botswana has demonstrated a solid commitment to responding to its HIV epidemic. We are the first country in the region to provide universal free antiretroviral treatment (ART) to people living with HIV, setting an example across the sub-Saharan African region. The impact of its treatment programme is widespread, and new infections have decreased significantly.

I know first-hand what it is like to lose close friends and relatives to this deadly virus. I lost my uncle, who was, funnily enough, a famous DJ in Francistown. He went by the name of DJ Cruz. Unfortunately, he passed away shortly after contracting the virus. I think I was about ten years old. I used to love watching him practise his turntables and scratch CDs and vinyl in preparation for his night gigs. Recently, my aunt Sipho, who was like our second mother, also passed away. Losing her was a massive blow to our family, especially to mum, because they were really close. Growing up, it became somewhat normal to have friends who lost either one or both parents to HIV/AIDS.

Therefore, my research and scriptwriting talents were vital to helping raise awareness as we collaborated with various charities and advocacy groups and the international charity organisation that funded this project. I remember us touring the country with the camera crew and research team. As we moved from village to village, we used questionnaires and conducted face-to-face interviews with individuals from different walks of life about this incredibly taboo subject. It was not an easy task for me, as I had to respectfully challenge beliefs and cultural norms to achieve my goal.

For example, there were times I struggled to articulate myself in front of an old lady in a rural village. She couldn't understand why I came knocking at her door with a piece of paper and a pen in my hand. She almost hit me with her walking stick because she misheard what I said. In trying to say in Setswana that I represented a company that addresses HIV/AIDS issues, she thought I said that our company is here to give her AIDS.

However, through continued discussions, I learned that a potent mixture of racism, poverty, and ignorance accelerated the spread of this incurable disease. Some believe that the idea of AIDS is a Western plot to weaken Africa or that the virus is some invention of the white man to curb black Africa's birth rate. Among the many other things we picked up, most people were misinformed about a recent campaign launched by the Ministry of Health, which asserted that circumcision prevented the transmission of HIV/AIDS by more than 60%. To the locals and most village men, that message implied that as long as the rate was greater than 50%, there was zero risk of contracting the virus. At the time, I was the first person in the media to discover this misconception.

Our team prepared and analysed collected data to present to different stakeholders. Together with my team, we organised meetings and public forums to present our findings and alert the public. We even managed to reach people such as ministers and other political figures and convinced them to act. In a lightbulb moment, I also incorporated this into our script and came up with the idea of casting local actors for the television drama. As a result of our work, the Ministry of Health revised its campaigns and published our reports. Within months of its airing on television, a decline in new HIV/AIDS infections was reported. I could not have been happier! One of the things I am passionate about is helping through campaigns and projects that help curb the spread of HIV/Aids.

With that being said, though, I wish I could erase some of the embarrassing moments I had during the early stages of this HIV/AIDS campaign project. Nothing could have prepared me for what was about to happen. I remember we were going from door to door conducting questionnaires with the locals in the villages. This time, we were somewhere deep in Botswana's Kalahari Desert. If you have seen Top Gear: Botswana Special with Jeremy Clarkson, Richard Hammond, and James May, those are the kinds of surroundings we were in. We drove through some of those localities and experienced similar challenges to the ones they did with their cars whilst trying to reach our preferred destination. Eventually, we stopped at one of the remote villages to conduct our research. Keep in mind that most people in this area couldn't speak or understand English. I mainly spoke English in towns and cities. So, this time, things were going to be very different, as you will soon find out. I had to switch to speaking Setswana, which, despite being my mother tongue, I can struggle with. I am used to speaking the more casual version of Setswana, which is widely spoken today, mainly by millennials. Therefore, asking me to observe the formal and more respectful way of speaking Setswana was a bit of a stretch. In fact, my understanding of formal Setswana is so bad that I got an F for my GCSE Setswana. So that should tell you all you need to know.

Anyway, despite the language barrier, I was assigned to carry out the research with a co-worker who had a better grasp of Setswana as well as the local dialect. Upon arrival, we started conducting questionnaires in public spaces and then extended our charitable work from house to house. At one point, I don't know what came over me, but I insisted that I would take the lead on the next mud hut that we were approaching. And so I tried; in accordance with traditional Setswana etiquette, I knocked and announced our arrival as we entered the yard. This is so that the house owner can come out and meet you at the gate or front yard to welcome you into their home. Or it could be to guard against uninvited guests dropping in on you just at the opportune point where you are dishing out food. Sometimes Batswana are not big on sharing scarce food with greedy neighbours—oh, the irony!

"Ko Ko! Dumelang!"I greeted formally. (Knock knock! Hello!)

Le teng mo lwapeng? (Anybody home?)

Ee re teng ka kwano. (Yes, we are here)

Le tsogile jang? (How are you?)

Ee, re tsogile mong wame, Ehee! Mme hela, nnete ya boammaruri ke gore hela ga rea tsoga mong wame"

(Yes, we are well, chief. Ok! But the truth of the matter is we are not well, chief.)

Ehee. Ehee!

Ok! Ok!

MICHAEL BANTU-KHOE

I know what you are already thinking, is this whole back and forth necessary? No, not really, but culturally, it is considered rude to jump into the purpose of your visit without first enquiring about the house owner's wellbeing. It's no wonder cold callers are not common in Botswana. Can you imagine how high their phone bill would be? It would be so frustrating for the telemarketers because by the time they got to the point of what they wanted to discuss; they would be so worn out they would be ready to die a thousand deaths.

I think Batswana have to be the only people in the world who don't seem to be fazed by these long-winded greetings. However, there's always a limit for every person. If you are not careful, some of these formal greetings can stretch for a good 10-15 minutes. And it took me roughly that long before things started to go a bit funny. After asking about the house owner's health and wellbeing, as well as asking after his family and domestic animals, then and only then, could I proceed to the introductions and the purpose of our visit.
So, racing against time, I started introducing myself and my co-worker. Speaking politely in Setswana, I said,

(Ntate) Sir, my name is Michael, and this is my friend and co-worker so and so. May I take your name, please?"

The house owner looked at us, responding in Setswana, *"Nxaham."*

I cannot lie, there must have been a good 30-second pregnant pause. I assumed he didn't hear the question I asked, so I repeated it in Setswana and just to be sure, this time a bit louder.

"Sir, what is your name?"

He repeated, *"Nxaham"*

It took a while to register that a word did come out of his mouth because we both thought he just yawned and would soon tell us his name. But nothing came; there was dead silence! I immediately thought, "Wait a minute, could he have a speech impediment?" That's possible, but then 15 minutes ago he sounded perfectly fine.

Whilst the three of us looked puzzled, my co-worker interjected, asking him the same question in Setswana but differently this time. It was something like, "Sir, what are you called?" The guy did the same thing; we could see his lips moving, and somehow, that movement turned into a yawn. But this time, a much bigger, louder yawn. "Nxaham!"

It was at that very moment that it started to dawn on us that, indeed, the yawn-like name, "Nxaham/Nxaha" was his given name. It is actually a common name amongst the Khoisan tribe in Botswana, who are the indigenous peoples of Southern Africa. It was clear that neither myself nor my co-worker had ever come across such a name. I feel bad thinking I almost laughed at him. That is just plain wrong to do in front of his face, let alone on his property. It would have been complete and utter disrespect, worthy of a trial by combat.

So, I pat myself on the back for holding the snicker in a bit longer until we had finished and had walked quite a distance from his house before letting it all out. My co-worker's reaction was the same. In fact, I think she was worse than me. At one point, I saw tears rolling down her face as she tried desperately not to laugh. And you know how you do that thing where you look at each other, fighting the urge to burst out laughing so badly while at the same time composing yourself, covering your mouth with your hand, and taking deep breaths so you don't inappropriately guffaw in mid-sentence? We were fighting a losing battle, holding our breaths to avoid splitting our sides in hysterics. But thankfully, neither of us gave in to our emotions at the time. It was really hard to keep a straight face and be professional after hearing something that funny. I was this close to cracking up and bursting into fits of uncontrolled laughter.

In retrospect, I never thought karma could be so relentless. I mean, it's not like being the butt of a joke or anything, but when you're branded with an alias that people laugh about for years and then get steamrolled by their own bad juju? That takes some doing! Soon after the Nxaham incident, I got to experience first-hand what it is like to be the butt of a joke courtesy of your moniker. And the person laughing at the pronunciation of my last name didn't have the decency to laugh in private but brazenly did it to my face! Would you believe that? Somebody, please hold me back! I beg you! before I commit a crime.

MICHAEL BANTU-KHOE

IF YOU
DON'T LAUGH
YOU'LL CRY

MICHAEL BANTU-KHOE

There are many emotions that come with being in love. One of the most common is nostalgia, because we often remember those early days when everything felt so perfect and hilarious all at once—like it did back then with my wife! I find myself listening to "Is This Love" by Bob Marley whenever I feel nostalgic about my relationship and reminisce about the first time I fell

MICHAEL BANTU-KHOE

in love with my wife. It might seem random, but this song just takes me down memory lane to the many romantic cheap dates we had in the first flush of our love characterised by late-night movies, parties and gatherings. If you have ever been in love with your significant other, then you most likely know the feeling that Bob Marley was alluding to.

However, finding that feeling of true love, let alone getting a suitable companion in this day and age can be as hard as finding a needle in a haystack. It's not impossible, but really, what are your chances of finding a tiny little thing in a pile of hay? The dating poll has become even more sophisticated. You now have to tick a lot of boxes to be in with the slightest whiff of a chance of someone swiping right for you and not left. Unless you choose not to play by the rules of the game and possess some kind of magnetic pull to help you locate the needle and attract the very thing you are looking for.

I, for one, didn't have such a magnetic pull. I didn't have what I thought at the time, were the right looks. I was frail and looked like I could be swept away by the blowing wind at any moment. I was no doubt influenced by the popular norm amongst some Batswana locals; that of waiting until you are financially stable and acquired some wealth before committing to a long-term relationship and marriage.

A part of me used that reasoning to deny myself the opportunity of pursuing real love and a long-term relationship. Could that be the reason why some of my countrymen wait until their mid-30s and in some cases, early 40s, before tying the knot? I don't know. But as a young man in my early twenties, I felt like I didn't have the kind of financial stability needed to maintain a relationship let alone start a family. I was too broke with no money or savings. My so-called music career was long dead, and I was no longer famous, I was back to being a nobody. Hence why to this day, I still struggle to understand what my wife saw in me. The very attributes I thought made a man more attractive to women, I did not possess at the time. And yet I ended up getting to know and eventually marry the love of my life. We met through mutual friends, and like any other romantic story, it begins with the guy thinking that the girl is way above his league. Which she was and still is.

You know when people say love is blind. If you saw me back then, you would have to have been blind in both eyes to agree to go on a few dates let alone fall in love with me. But I credit her for her bravery. If I'm honest, my wife kind of reminds me of my mum in the sense that they are both very loving, loyal and hospitable. When I tell you that this woman has been with me through thick and thin, I mean it. Shortly after we met, I became jobless, and she kept us going. I think it takes a certain type of man to admit that. Even amid my many failed hustles, I can rightfully say I was blessed to have somebody as patient as her. I always laugh when I tell people that, when my wife and I both hit rock bottom, at one point we were forced to downsize and live together in a studio apartment where the bedroom was also the kitchen, the living room and dining area.

Thankfully we had an indoor toilet that was adjacent to both the washing machine and wall wardrobes. Even as a university dropout and failed architect, I could see the many flaws of this property. And yet it was what we could afford at the time.

When things eventually improved, I set up a date for us and on bended knee, popped the question. I was so over the moon when she said yes! I couldn't have been any happier. And I was like great, let's do this. But then, there was a slight problem. I had to make this official and travel all the way to the UK to ask her parents for their daughter's hand in marriage. That looked so easy on paper until I met the dad and on first impressions; learning that he owned a gym explained why, to me, he looked like he could snap me into pieces with a simple handshake if he wanted to.

Knowing who I am and what I was like, I immediately chickened out and suggested to my girlfriend that we elope and break the news to both our parents on our way to our honeymoon. That sounded like a good idea, but you'll be happy to learn that she immediately shot down the idea and pleaded with me to ask her father before the news of our intent to get engaged leaked out. So, I started planning the best time to carry out this mission impossible of trying to get her father's blessings and at the same time, planning an escape route in case things didn't go as planned, and I had to flee to safety.

In retrospect, I wish I could go back in time and tell myself; you have nothing to fear, the man is just a gentle giant who happens to own a gym. I would definitely have parked the breaks on what I was thinking at the time and not lost sleep over it. My fear was well-founded on the following logical reason. Do you know how two people can have different interpretations of the same thing or interpret the same message differently? For example, let's say you approach a film director and say to them, *"You really want to shoot a pilot,"* they might turn around and say yeah sure go ahead and do it. You can use my camera while you are at it. But if you repeat the same comment to an air hostess or airport security guard whilst boarding your flight, you risk getting tackled down like a quarter-back and arrested for saying *"you really want to shoot a pilot"*. You could even face a prison sentence depending on the country you are in.

And that's my point! Do you now understand why I was in such a panic? Things can get messy really quickly. Just because my lovely girlfriend agrees to marry me, her dad might not approve of me and thus, want to kill me, which I would totally understand. If the shoe were on the other foot and I had a daughter and somebody came in to ask for my blessing to marry her, I would crush them into pieces right then and there. I would no doubt give the boyfriend a tough time and treat him like the infamous "Reggie scene" from the movie Bad Boys 2. I am sure many dads with daughters empathise and glorify Martin Lawrence's behaviour in that movie.

Luckily for me, there wasn't any physical assault or threats at gunpoint even though I'd expected it. I was thrilled when he gave me his blessing. I was indeed welcomed into the family, and they treated me like one of their own. Even then, I couldn't help but think of how weddings or marriage in general, is conducted and treated differently here in the UK than back home in Botswana. You see, in Botswana, everybody knows that if you are contemplating marriage, the most important thing you should do is determine whether you can afford to pay "Lobola", commonly known as the bride price. This, my friend, is a make-or-break traditional practice that goes as far back as I can remember. The bride price is commonly practised throughout many tribes and nations around the world. Botswana didn't invent it, but rather, we perfected it into a well-oiled money-making machine. Like most things, what started off as a kind gesture from the groom's side of the family, has transformed into a winning lottery ticket for some in the bride's family.

Of course, not all traditional lobola practices are inherently evil or degrading as some would think. Some families are happy to follow the same traditions of old and just view them for what they are. Whereas some take advantage of the prospect of getting rich, and you often hear or read stories of husbands who end up abusing their wives, claiming they had paid for them and thus, view their wives as possessions.

What I also dislike about the practice is seeing a poor young couple being exploited by greedy uncles and relatives in some cases, because they are the ones who often benefit the most from these sorts of arrangements. In some areas, it is common knowledge that the uncles tend to get the largest share of the bride price. That is because traditionally, they are tasked with the privilege of handing the bride to the groom. I am so glad that I didn't have to contend with all that. But that doesn't stop my father-in-law from jokingly asking me for his cows, goats, chickens and a good portion of the bride price for his daughter. My answer to him is always the same. I tell him that it's near impossible for us to ship all the cows, goats and sheep from Botswana to the UK. The poor animals wouldn't survive the long arduous journey.

I often wondered though how much of the total bride price money would my wife be worth. I know she will punch me in the arm for saying this, but I just want to calculate the price for the sake of knowing. I mean, I know how much bride price contributions were made for my sisters. From the inside information, I once gathered from a drunk uncle, I was able to get a clear picture of how some of the negotiations with the groom's families were carried out, including the valuations.

My uncle said the pricing criteria differs slightly from tribe to tribe. But what often increases the price or number of cattle and livestock is how well educated the bride is. Does she have a university degree, Masters or PHD or is she uneducated, holding a GCSE certificate or high school diploma? The other thing, which is probably the most obvious; does she have any children outside of this proposed marriage? If yes, then the price drops slightly. If not, then we're potentially looking at a small fortune. Mind you, the same rule applies to the groom. If he is marrying the mother of his kids, he has to pay a hefty price, or a penalty of sorts charged for each child conceived outside wedlock. That's what my dad had to pay.

I believe he had eight children outside wedlock before he decided to officially tie the knot with mum. Good thing he didn't wait any longer because 12 children would amount to way too many cows to give to another family. And for someone like him who was very fond of cattle, he would have begrudgingly given them away and lost a lot of sleep over it.

So having considered everything and taken account of the pros and cons; my beloved wife is presumably worth a lot. She and I went shopping for an engagement ring and as soon as we found one, we immediately announced our engagement to our friends and family. We both didn't want to wait too long to get married, so we agreed to set the wedding date six months from the time of our engagement. Just enough time to get both of my parents and *the eleven disciples* over to the UK to come and celebrate our wedding with us. Now, that's what would have happened in an ideal world. However, before I can even tell you about the inevitable family drama that soon followed from my Botswana side of the family, let me start first with the positives. And what better way to start than the bachelor party?

While the ladies travelled to Greece for their Bridal shower, I went to visit some friends in London. Bear in mind that the only time I'd been to the city was when I was travelling in and out of the country going through Heathrow airport, so I never really got to explore inner-city London. What I didn't know though, was that my London friends had already planned a surprise bachelor party AKA stag do. For spoilers, this wasn't your typical bachelor party marked with a wild party complete with strippers and naked bodies everywhere. That was off the table, but man kudos to the lads because what they pulled off was unforgettable and a lot more exciting.

So, I woke up at my friends' apartment in Camden. And for those of you who don't know where that is, it's one of the hip, cool, cosmopolitan, funky town with an eclectic mix of markets, cuisines and live music venues where back in those days, you could easily bump into the rich and famous. The celebrities would sometimes be seen walking their dogs or exercising, jogging or driving their expensive cars. So, you can imagine what it must have felt like for me to be there. For a village boy like me who grew up surrounded by mud huts, donkeys and goats roaming freely in the streets, Camden felt like a serious upgrade.

By the way, if you have never spent a night in a thatched mud hut, I highly recommend it. In my opinion, it is such a phenomenally humbling experience worth experiencing at least once in your lifetime. Try it, and you will thank me later!

MICHAEL BANTU-KHOE

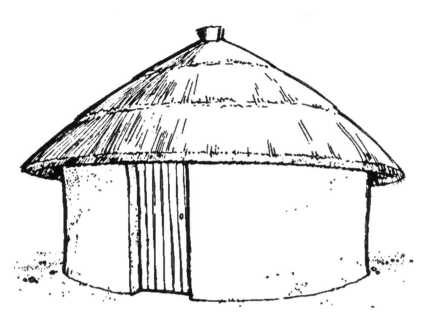

An African thatched mud hut

Anyway, back to the bachelor party. So, I got up in the morning around 10 am and to my surprise, the house was dead silent. There was no one else in the apartment except me. I mean, I knocked and checked every room, and the house was empty. I remember thinking, "Did everyone just go to work or something?" Wait a minute, it's the weekend, and none of my friends works during weekends. Plus, they would have told me if they were.

MICHAEL BANTU-KHOE

So, I went to where I left my phone charging and grabbed it to reach out to my friends, but all my calls went to voicemail. I tried every number on my phone, but none of my London friends picked up. I started getting a bit suspicious, but then I thought, maybe they went out to get breakfast. So, as I sat on the couch and reached to grab the TV remote on the side table and stumbled upon an envelope with my name on it. The words on the front said, "Please look inside."

I gently tore the envelope open, and a random key fell out. Inside the envelope, there were a few other items enclosed. There was a handwritten letter with what looked like a list of instructions and clues written on it. Also attached to the letter was an oyster card with my name on it and a few coins. I immediately knew that these guys were up to something, but what was it? I was soon to find out. I carefully read and re-read the letter. And the more I read it, it sounded like a treasure hunt map with intriguing puzzles. The instructions laid out required me to travel around London city collecting clues and solving mysteries, and in the end, I was promised something beyond extraordinary. I remember panicking and feeling excited at the same time. Even while taking a shower and getting ready for what lay ahead, I was buzzing with excitement and curiously looking forward to the challenge. Looking back, it felt like I was acting out a script from a thriller movie with lots of suspense; the kind that keeps you on the edge of your seat. In fact, according to my friends, this entire mystery game was inspired by the BBC hit TV series, Sherlock Holmes, with Benedict Cumberbatch and co-star Martin Freeman. They knew I was a massive fan, so I give them credit for mimicking my favourite show.

Before embarking on the challenge, the first instruction was to use the key enclosed to lock the apartment on my way out. And that was obviously easy enough, but the rest of the challenges that soon followed were nowhere near as easy as the first task. Let me explain! As mentioned earlier, one of the riddles or instructions had me travelling from one part of the city to the next. Keep in mind that, for a Londoner, this task would be easy peasy. However, for a foreigner, and one who'd never been to London at that, navigating the bus routes and train maps is not my cup of tea. I guess what also didn't help was the fact that I also got a C in GCSE Geography, proving that my sense of direction is not the most reliable. I am no use travelling by myself, especially using the London underground, switching train lines and winding my way through the city. I wish I had told my friends about my lacking sense of direction before all this. But then again, how could I have known what surprise they had in store for me?

Thankfully, I somehow managed to find my way towards the city centre to a specific Waterstones. Inside the Waterstones bookstore, I had to locate a certain aisle in a specific book section. In that section, I had to find the right shelf and count the order of books to a specific number. After doing all of that, I finally located the book they wanted me to find. It was one of my favourites, a Sherlock Holmes novel by Arthur Conan Doyle. I had to turn the novel to a certain page number, and as I opened the page, there was a £20 note stuck to it and another letter in an envelope with the next instructions. The sticky note attached said I should buy the book with the money and use the change to tip the cashier. That then made me think he was in on this whole idea, and the tip was actually payment for his cooperation. Brilliant, I thought! So, the next quest was to head off to one of London's tourist attractions,

MICHAEL BANTU-KHOE

Trafalgar Square. Once I got there, I can't remember clearly, but I think I had to locate a certain monument and count about 10 steps towards the water fountain all while looking for an X-mark on the pavement. It took me several tries, but eventually, I found it. I must have looked ridiculous to onlookers who probably thought I was a mad man.

Once I found the X, I had to follow the arrows drawn on the pavement, leading me off towards an area I had no clue about at the time. Just to show you how insane this was, I had to cross several streets with lots of busy oncoming traffic, cyclists and many pedestrians walking through the busy city. Imagine walking through all that commotion while meandering down the pavement looking for arrows drawn in chalk. I was pretty much an accident waiting to happen. Luckily, I survived as I came to the end of the street, where my friends wanted me to be. All of a sudden, I heard a phone ringing, but strangely, it wasn't mine. It came from an old K6 or red telephone box that I was standing next to. To be honest, at first, I didn't know what to do. So, I looked around to see if anybody would come and answer the phone, but no one except me seemed to

notice the phone ringing. Something told me to answer
it. So, I hesitantly crept towards the phone booth,
slowly picked up the phone and said, "Hello!"
As soon as, I answered, I could hear somebody
laughing wickedly from the other end, "Muahahaha." It
was menacing, just like Dr Evil from Austin powers. I
can't lie, hearing that coming from one of my friends
drove me into a frenzy. I wish you could have seen me;
I was behaving like Colin Farrell as the publicist Stu
Shepard when he found himself trapped in a *phone
booth*, pinned down by an extortionist's caller with a
sniper rifle. I believe my friends had neither of those
weapons pointed up at me, thank God! But the way they
kept stalking me with their watchful eyes, felt even
scarier. Apparently, they had been following me all day
from a distance, all disguised to blend in with the
public.

Finally, I got an instruction over the phone to read
another clue hidden underneath the phone box. It had a
ticket to a water taxi that took me on a boat cruise
across the river Thames. I really enjoyed that a lot and
while cruising through the waters I could see my friends
waving at me from the bridge up top as I swooped

underneath in the water taxi. Luckily, they were filming me enjoying myself and waving back at them. It took me a while to reach the final task and I was happy that it ended up with us all gathered together laughing and dining at a Sherlock Holmes pub in St James's right there in the city of London. That, my friend, was how I got intellectually bested AKA "Sherlocked" which became the highlight of what led to one of the happiest days of my life, my wedding.

That being said, let me digress and fill you in on what almost drove me nuts a few days before that special event. Once again, my family in Botswana did what they always do best, make a mockery of me. When I first broke the news on the twelve disciples WhatsApp group, I swear to you, at one point I woke up to like 100 messages on my phone, with everyone making grand promises, declaring that they were going to book tickets to travel to the UK for my wedding. The gullible side of me was totally sold on the dream. I even got emotional thinking about it and how awesome it would be. To see both my mum and dad and the eleven, gathered around on my happiest day. But no, that's not how it went down. When we got closer and closer to the wedding day, even then, I was met with more talk and less action. Everyone kept saying they were coming and that I should reserve them a seat at the wedding reception, but no one was booking any flights or enquiring about anything. But I had no reason to believe that they couldn't come. This was way before COVID-19, so there wasn't any restriction on travel. And it's not like the tickets were unaffordable; I knew my older siblings had money and stable jobs. Plus, they all had six months to plan; it's not like I was forcing or begging them. They could easily have pulled out and said sorry bro, we can't make it, and I would happily have accepted it. But no, they kept on promising me and my wife that they would make it to the wedding.

I wish I had given up hope to save me time to focus on planning the actual wedding itself. I don't know why I was so oblivious because back home there is a common saying that Batswana are a nation of people who find it hard to say "no". You see, they would rather lie to you and say they will do something, knowing very well that they won't do it. Saying "no" to someone's face is deemed even far more offensive and disrespectful than failing to make good on your promise.

MICHAEL BANTU-KHOE

And to make matters worse, in Setswana, we have no singular noun for the word "lie", but rather, we have the plural version, "lies/maaka". The idea is that when someone tells a lie, they must then tell another lie to compensate for the first lie, and then another lie to compensate for that lie, and so on. So, before you know it, you're surrounded by a web of lies.

That's exactly what happened to my siblings at the time. They made up all sorts of stories and lied so many times about travelling to the UK for my wedding, and I was so naive that I believed every single one of them without any hesitation. So, less than a week before the wedding, out of the eleven people invited by both of my parents, only one managed to book a flight to the UK. Literally days before the big day. It was my little brother, and his itinerary showed that he was due to land in the country at Heathrow airport on the day of the wedding. Then he'd have to bus it for the next three hours to arrive in time for the wedding ceremony. Luckily, we planned to start everything in the afternoon, so my little brother just about made it to the wedding reception but missed seeing us exchange the vows. That, to me, was the epitome of arriving at your destination in African time. I can't lie, I was very angry, but when I saw him in the flesh, we both couldn't hold back the tears as we hugged. I was so happy that at least somebody from my family made it.

We held the wedding reception at a local vineyard, and what I liked about it besides the epic scenic views was that the owners had organised to have llamas and alpacas dressed in bow ties, greeting everyone at the entrance as they came in. We had such a great time, and the weather on the day was delightful, one of the hottest days of the year, which according to British weather standards, was lush! The rest of the evening went by so quickly, and everyone around us was so happy, I just wished the rest of my family were there to share the excitement and precious moment in my life. But either way, I knew they were with me in spirit. The following day, we packed our bags, said our goodbyes and flew somewhere nice for our honeymoon. We went to Jersey, a small island in the English Channel located just 19 miles off the French coast. Many islets make up the Channel Islands, so besides Jersey, we visited other areas such as Guernsey, Alderney, Sark, Herm, Jethou and Brechou.

MICHAEL BANTU-KHOE

On returning from our honeymoon, we decided to spend the first two years of our married life back home in Botswana. Those two years flew by. And soon enough, we were back at it again. Having squandered all our savings and being in and out of jobs left us with only one option. With a heavy heart, we took the tough decision to say goodbye to Botswana, leaving behind friends and family to go somewhere we thought the grass would be greener. *(Aka Greener Pastures)*.

MICHAEL BANTU-KHOE

DON'T YOU LAUGH! IT'S NOT FUNNY

MICHAEL BANTU-KHOE

In 1652, the Dutch first established a settlement in the Cape in South Africa. Originally intended as a mere stop for ships on route to the Dutch East Indies, it later witnessed an invasion of settlers, from the Netherlands, France, Germany and Britain. These lands, however, were already inhabited, and it wasn't long before tensions between locals and settlers erupted. I was standing near one of the Dutch harbour where some of

MICHAEL BANTU-KHOE

these Dutch ships would have set sail. I found myself again relocated overseas, but this time with a companion. As stated in the last chapter, I had married the love of my life.

We told each other when we first began dating that before we decided to settle and start having a family, our goal would be to travel across the world together as much as we can. The pact we made with one another led us on a crazy adventure that looking back, I don't know how we just about managed to survive. After spending a significant amount of time in Botswana. We ended up opting to reside someplace in Europe as a result of one of these travels. The Netherlands was chosen for two reasons. First, it was simpler to get visas, and second, the other half of my wife's family is Dutch. So, her Rotterdammer grandmother, whom we call 'Oma,' is Dutch. She was just eleven years old when the Nazis, led by Hitler, dropped the first bomb on Rotterdam.

When we were first dating we promised each other that before we started a family, though, we agreed that after spending a considerable amount of time in Botswana,

MICHAEL BANTU-KHOE

we would travel together around the world. It was through one of these journeys that we ended up deciding to live somewhere in Europe. We chose the Netherlands for two reasons. Firstly, it was easier to enter in terms of getting visas, and secondly, the other side of my wife's family is Dutch. So yeah, her Dutch grandmother, whom we call 'Oma', is a Rotterdammer. She was only ten years old when the Nazis under Hitler first dropped a bomb on the city of Rotterdam.

The Netherlands became my second home, and I truly loved it. I enjoyed the scenic beauty of the cities, towns and the villages on the outskirts with greenhouses and tulip farms, surrounded by well-constructed dikes and traditional windmills and good roads and cycling paths. It was mind-blowing. I remember seeing older people on their bikes – grandmas and grandpas pedalling, racing and zooming through the bike lanes, and thinking to myself that there is no way in hell my grandmother would do that. No wonder their older population is fitter than those in other countries. Dutch people, in general, are pretty friendly, pleasant and hospitable. Their food and culture are also exciting experiences. I really felt at peace and, to some degree, welcome in their country.

We rented a one-bedroom apartment in the middle of the harbour city of Rotterdam. Rotterdam, often referred to as the gateway to Europe, has the world's largest port. I liked how multicultural and prosperous the city was. For jobs, my wife, who is a trained chef, landed a cooking job at one of The Hague's daycare schools. I struggled to find a job, and eventually started my own cleaning business. I remember cycling back and forth to clients within Rotterdam and taking the trains to do one-off cleaning jobs in cities like Amsterdam, Delft, The Hague, Leiden and Utrecht.

It was a lot harder to find an office job, partly because the requirements were that you had to be fluent in spoken and written Dutch. We both took mandatory Dutch lessons, and my wife was progressing a bit faster than I was. She said that her Dutch grandmother, or Oma, used to read her Dutch stories when she was little, so picking up the language was slightly more manageable for her. I, on the other hand, struggled desperately. I suck at languages, to be honest. The only

MICHAEL BANTU-KHOE

advantage I had, which I didn't realise at the time, was when I found myself up against the wrong crowd or encountered racists who yelled racist slurs and verbally attacked me. Although I could still see and sense the intent and hatefulness in their eyes, my inability to understand the local language saved me. I had the rare privilege of not being affected by their hurtful words because I had no clue what they were on about. It felt like I had on a bulletproof, No-To-Racism shield. And the more I looked unaffected by the hate speech aimed at me, the angrier they got. As long as they never laid their hands on me, it kept me in high spirits and feeling my regular self.

Although not entirely exempt from the systemic and institutionalised form of racism, winning small daily battles at ground level reassures us that the war against racism and discrimination can be won in a much distant future, but realistically not in my lifetime. I remember watching a stand-up comedy routine by the South African comedian and *The Daily Show* host, Trevor Noah. He made an interesting point about how the word "Nigga" is often used to oppress Black people in America, but ironically, that same word, when used against black people in some parts of Africa, does not carry the same weight. I recall the first time I was ever called the N-word and at the same time not feeling offended by it, only because it came from an unusual source. I think the films and movies we watched on TV had us believe that hate crime is exclusively between black and white people. However, my encounter, believe it or not, happened while I was shopping in a busy China town in Malaysia. Hearing that coming from an Asian person didn't hurt per se, I was more confused than offended. It happened between me and a bunch of local shopkeepers. As always, I was involved in a price tug of war for some knock off designer trainers, and the longer the negotiations went on, the more frustrated the shopkeeper became. I wasn't budging on my offer, but I think the last straw was my final offer. The shopkeeper went berserk, threatening us as he kicked us out of his shop. And it was in that moment that he looked at me and uttered the word N****.

Surprisingly, I wasn't affected in any way, and to show how powerless his insults were to me, I burst out laughing and so did my Batswana friends who were with me. Other shopkeepers nearby caught wind of what was happening and saw we were not reacting the way they expected black people to react, totally at odds with what happens in the movies whenever they are called the N-word. They started spewing anything black-related.

For example, one of the guys said this right to my face with the loudest voice you can imagine, "Hakuna Matata!!" "Hakuna Matata!!" while the others chanted, "Barak Obama!!!"

Aargh, I wish I had recorded that; it would have gone viral even in those days. The experience just made us laugh all the more. We were literally all in tears of laughter, gasping for breath as we walked off. That was my *friendly encounter* with racism.

Each piece of the African continent may have its own derogatory term it uses to denigrate black people. Still, the question remains, how do you cause generations of people to unlearn a hateful and demeaning word? I got to a point where in order to feel comfortable in any place I visited outside Rotterdam, I would have to play a game called "spot the black". It's pretty easy and self-explanatory. All I had to do was spot a black person and start counting. If I counted more than ten black people in the space of only a few minutes, then I knew I was in a safe zone. If however, I struggled to find even two or three black people, I would start getting uncomfortable, and I knew I had to be quick with whatever I was doing and leave.

Before you judge me, white people, understand these two things. First: go easy on me with those comments because I may or may not have a heart condition. Second: some white people do it as well when they visit Africa. Maybe during a safari tour, you can see the excitement in their faces whenever they see other white tourists from other countries. It's like folks from long-lost families meeting for the first time. I also like doing 'the nod' whenever I see or cross paths with my fellow African brothers and sisters. The 'black nod' is more than just a greeting. It's a special moment where two black people stop for a moment, and without uttering a word, appreciate each other's blackness, and congratulate each other for having made it this far. I live for that moment. Sometimes when another black person doesn't return the black nod, I feel offended; it's almost as if they insulted me.

All giggling aside, I really love visiting The Netherlands and interacting with Dutch people. Despite being very direct and obsessed with their bicycles, I grew fond of them. Dutch people have a great sense of humour, and there are many new things you can learn just by visiting the country. For example, did you know that cats can get AIDS? See? I didn't realise this until a Dutch friend told me that her cat died of AIDS. I really couldn't keep a straight face when I heard that. Being African, I thought AIDS was "our thing" but not anymore, I guess. If you ever get a chance to visit, I suggest you first go on a city tour.

When my Missus and I went to Amsterdam, we booked one of those city tours, which was freaking amazing. If you haven't done it before, I suggest you do it when you visit. The tour group comprised tourists from all over the world. Our tour guide was excellent and knew her Dutch history inside out – so much so that many of us tipped her well at the end. She took us on a walk that started not far from Justin Bieber's incredible new three-storey, £22m pad in the heart of Amsterdam.

She showed us all the monuments and old church buildings dating as far back as the 1600s. She also took us through the famous red-light district, where half-naked women pose in the windows. Luckily enough, I never saw a thing because I was too busy looking at my wife. We then went past the coffee shops. At first, I didn't realise they are found across the Netherlands and sell weed only and have nothing to do with actual coffee. I looked stupid, asking for a black coffee with no sugar in these so-called 'cafés'. I must admit, it was the first time ever I saw a white person with dreadlocks. Towards the end of the tour, our guide shared some aspects of Dutch history with us, which resonated with me.

Apparently, a long time ago, the Dutch didn't have surnames or family names; they only used first names. But later, during the 1800s, when the French occupied The Netherlands, Napoleon, the French emperor, forced the Dutch to adopt family names for tax purposes. The Dutch thought this would just be a temporary thing, so you know what they did? They took on comical and offensive-sounding names as a practical joke on their French occupiers. So whenever a French official called out their names, the Dutch would laugh hysterically. Little did they know that these names would stick for centuries and be handed down to their descendants. Today it is, therefore, common to encounter inappropriate last names such as:

Piper / Pijpers (To fellate someone)

Poepjes (Little Crap/sh*t)

Rotmensen (Rotten people)

Piest (to urinate)

Paardebek (Horse's mouth)

Eikel/acorn means the head of the penis (dick in English).

Meneer Eikel (Mr Dickhead)

Van de Kloot (from the balls)

Now, if you're Dutch and feel offended by me saying this, I sincerely apologise. My intentions were not to hurt your feelings but to show you how much in common we have. Yes, like some of you, I have an unspellable last name that I have been made fun of all my life. And if I'm honest with you, there have been times in my life when I have thought about changing my last name to something more anglicised, not only for me to fit in but also to get a call back for an interview or something. You see, sometimes, when life hits you really hard, and you're constantly knocked down, you find yourself feeling desperate and in despair every now and then. I am talking about the point where you have hit rock bottom, and you don't see any other way out of your distressing situation. At that point, it's so damn easy for you to start compromising your morals and disown who you really are. In my case, being unemployed for years took its toll on me. I felt pressure to change who I was, my identity, my name, just so I could get a decent, well-paying job and be accepted by society. However, depending on each person's circumstance, I know that this may be easier said than done.

When our colonisers first hit the shores of Southern Africa, they renamed my beloved country, Botswana, Bechuanaland, a much more palatable term for *them*, not us. It became a lot easier to see why for generations, many are still psychologically conditioned to want to have Westernised and English sounding names. I say this now, but I have previously considered changing my last name to "Wildberry". I figured if only I could do a play on words and translate my Setswana surname into English, then my conscience would be at peace. At the time, I thought it was a brilliant idea. In that way, I could still technically retain my name and get a decent job without voluntarily taking on a shared or slave master's name.

Does that make any sense? Take for example the country Holland. Some people call it The Netherlands while others call it Holland, we are all referring to the same place. Why can't I have a second name like that? Because think of how people in different parts of the world refer to this particular tropical fruit. Some call it passionfruit, while others call it granadilla. 90 per cent of the time, we're referring to the same juicy fruit. I wanted to mix things up and possibly change my last name like that. Why would that not be acceptable? I do not know. A much better example I can think of is the various ways in which people pronounce the name Jesus. Depending on where you are from, that name is spelt and pronounced differently but refers to the same person. So I wanted something similar to my last name.

MICHAEL BANTU-KHOE

Unfortunately, I am not as popular as Jesus. Not only that, both of my parents would be sick to the stomach if one day I said to them that they can now start addressing me as Mr Wildberry. I would be pronounced dead the following day.

So with me not going ahead with the name change, it meant that I had to live with whatever challenges or struggles came with bearing a foreign-sounding name in working Britain. For the record, my official government last name is *"Maretlwaneng"*. I've been teased about the "click-click noise" in the middle (-tlw-) throughout my life. And to be fair, to the ears of Westerners, that clicky noise sounds like someone typing angrily on the keyboard or an angry cashier chewing their bubble-gum loudly. It's tough, white people, I know, but, unfortunately, names with clicking noises aren't tailor-made for your tongues. Actually, that's a lie. White people always make an effort to correctly pronounce names that are potentially Western. For example
Swarovski - Swor-off-ski,
Schwarzenegger - shworts-uh-neg-er
Stravinsky - Struh – vin - skee

MICHAEL BANTU-KHOE

But don't make an effort to pronounce the following correctly.

Ejiofor - edge-ee-oh-for

Aaliyah - aah-lee-ya

Look, it's okay to ask the person how to pronounce their name. Making assumptions can be really damaging to their careers/morale/health.

I remember being at the Dutch embassy in London and the lady behind the counter trying to read out loud the names on my passport. She was like:

"Goedmorgen *(which is good morning in Dutch)* Mr Michael Maretlyuyumyum"

It sounded like she was swallowing something bitter. And when she repeated it, it sounded like "marijuana". Mr Michael Marijuana. Ain't that something. We both chuckled at the attempt, but I didn't make a fuss because I've heard way worse. I do encounter foreigners who genuinely want to try to pronounce it correctly. I ask them to think of the name Marie Antoinette or Mark Twain. Both of the names kind of rhyme with my Setswana version, Maretlwaneng. But hang on a minute; before you tongue twist and butcher my surname, remember that, depending on how you pronounce it, you could unknowingly be swearing at people in my mother tongue, which can get you beaten up in countries like Botswana, Lesotho and South Africa. I say this because it has happened before. It becomes problematic whenever white people break it down and say it out in syllables, *as if teaching a child to say a long word in set phrases*. Much like if you try to pronounce the word *"assets"* and you go like *"ass"* - "sets*"*. It's that split-second pause after you say *"ass"*. If that happened to you during a presentation at work with all the top senior managers present, could you honestly say your heart wouldn't sink as you plodded along and fumbled through the remaining slides? That uncomfortable feeling you and your audience feel is what I experience ten times over whenever white people try to pronounce my last name in the following word groups, "Maret -lwan- eng". And if I am honest with you, I don't think my grandmother would let it slide. It just sounds obscene, especially when you say "Marete" with confidence, because it translates as "dick" or "penis" in Setswana.

So, you now understand why I always look away when people say it to my face; you're calling me a real dick!

MICHAEL BANTU-KHOE

And it gets worse. Some people repeat it over and over, trying their very best to get it right. But with every attempt, here is how it sounds like to me: *"Michael Maret, Marete, Penis, penis, penis, penis, penis, penis, penis, penis, penis…."* By the way, that would usually go on until I politely ask them to stop. Therefore before we agree to put this to bed, I have a special announcement for all my white friends and acquaintances. The next time you call me by my full name in public, please, please, I beg you, say it in one breath and don't pause or take breaths in the middle.

That being said, I do empathise with people with rude-sounding last names such as Seamen, Wiener or Woodcock. How about Aycock, Dick or Dicks? What if you had to change your last name to Cummings or Cockburn? The reality is, you would spend half of your life at work, on the phone with the IT guys asking them to keep an eye on your emails because the server keeps flagging them as porn spam. I bet they'll have a file on you with all the written warnings each time you try to type in your name. Or when someone refuses to take your order on the phone or RSVP you at a hotel because your last name is Dicks. Man, that must really hurt – no pun intended.

You see, in my culture, unlike the Dutch, the last name is bestowed upon you based on your outstanding quality. So, if Maretlwaneng means wild berries, that in itself already speaks volumes. I can now understand why my grandfather didn't want to tell us more about our family history – it was way too embarrassing. My great great great grandfather wasn't a hunter, he wasn't a tribal warrior, he was damn good at picking berries, I tell you. You must understand that from the history books we read at school, we learn that men were hunters and warriors, and women were gatherers of fruits during the time of our great ancestors. Those were the only two jobs available. So, for my great great great grandfather to make it into the fruit industry like that must have been quite an outstanding achievement. Either that, or he was a slave fruit picker! For the purpose of this book, I will go with the first option.

Do you know what that teaches me? That you have to dare to be different. Have the courage to live authentically, whether you are at work or anywhere

MICHAEL BANTU-KHOE

else, don't let the world define who you are or let it fit you into its mould. It's completely okay to be different. Embrace it. I have done more than that by choosing not to change my last name. Little did I know that what happened next would challenge the very essence of who I am.

———————————◆———————————

TAKE A WALK

IN MY SHOES

MICHAEL BANTU-KHOE

Growing up, my father taught us numerous life lessons using Setswana proverbs, idioms, and folklore. The one that truly resonated with me throughout the years, was the life lesson on self-acceptance and how to live your life while embracing your flaws. You may be wondering how you convey such a powerful lesson to a vulnerable young man. My father told me a folk tale

MICHAEL BANTU-KHOE

about a man who would carry two buckets every morning and evening to fetch drinking water from a well some distance away. Carrying two buckets of water all the way home was his everyday habit. He did, however, have a little issue. One of the buckets he was using had a small leak, and he had no way of replacing it or repairing the leak. When he was at the well, he would fill both buckets with water to the brim. By the time he reached his home, one bucket was still full, and the other was always half full. This clearly upset the man and gave him a lot of back pains due to the uneven weight he was carrying.

Anyway, this back and forth went on for a long time until one morning, the man woke up, gathered his buckets, and went to the well as usual. To his astonishment, he saw flowers blossoming along the same route he normally went. The water spilling from his bucket day after day continued watering the seeds that bloomed into flowers. And this made him very happy. The moral of this tale is rather obvious. Having a flaw does not imply that you are a lost cause. Everyone, in my opinion, has an individual weak spot or at least one area where they might improve, but it's up to you to decide whether you want to utilise that area as a strength or a weakness in your life. My father instilled in us an appreciation that certain flaws may sometimes result in positive outcomes in our lives. So, cheer-up young man, as my dad would often say, people will love you for embracing your perfect imperfections.

If I'm being really honest, as a perfectly imperfect human, I have more than a few flaws. For starters, let's begin with the one that's the least debatable. Although I may come off as articulate, English is not really my first language. So, at times, I will just blurt out things out of context the way a child does when learning to speak or using a new phrase in a sentence.

And speaking about humiliating gaffes. I was working as an entry-level employee in the UK at the time, earning a minimum wage. I've since risen through the ranks, but my previous role was mostly customer-facing, requiring me to make several phone calls to engage with customers and resolve their queries. I must admit that I struggled and felt apprehensive over the phone initially, and what's worse, my nerves led me to make some of the most cringeworthy and, at times, poor word choices.

The organisation had employed roughly a hundred of us. Since we were operating as a call centre, we were expected to hit the ground running. Almost all of the new hires in the facility had no previous experience answering phones in this fashion. It's something we all had to learn by trial and error. And by trial and error, I mean that no one understood what they were doing. We took months to perfect even the most basic tasks. It was one of those jobs that made you feel like you were drinking straight from a fire truck hose. Many of the new employees broke down in tears and quit shortly after having to deal with irate consumers over the phone.

I transferred from another department where I did administrative work and sent letters to customers. This job was a new challenge for me. I, like everyone else, made a lot of errors, but the good thing is that I learned from them. That being said, please do not take the following out of context since, one, I was still a newbie learning the job and, two, no one had taught us the proper way to do things. We simply had to just figure things out for ourselves.

As a result, I apologise in advance to those who may not find these cringe-worthy experiences amusing. It all started on a gloomy Monday morning. Everyone was tired and exhausted after the weekend, as one would expect. I remember having to dial a number for a company called FROZEN PUBS, which appeared in large capital letters on my computer screen. Without thinking twice, I took up the phone and told the person on the other end:

> "Hello, hi, good morning. My name is Michael. I'm calling from such-and-such company. May I please speak to the owner of the business called Frozen Pubes?"

That's how I pronounced it. The person on the phone was like, "What? Huh?" And I repeated myself for the second time, and a third time, each time raising my voice and confidently asking for the owner of "Frozen Pubes".

Finally, the person on the other end of the phone burst out laughing before graciously correcting me on how to pronounce their company name. I felt silly and dumb. To say the least, it had been a humiliating morning. Now, before you all come after me on social media, remember that in Africa, we don't call pubs "pubs". We call them "bars" or "shebeens". So, don't you laugh at me for my honest mistake! I think the language barrier has a part to play.

It wasn't the first time I mistook a word for something else or even blurbed the wrong word. But let me tell you about two of my most humiliating recent occurrences. One of my co-workers recently inquired, "How's my Baba?" Now, where I come from, the phrase is used to refer to someone elderly, such as your grandfather, but in the UK, it is used as a term of endearment to refer to a baby or toddler. You can image how stupid I looked when I told the colleague that I appreciated his concern, but he was no longer with us. "He's been dead for almost a decade now." As you could imagine, there was a great deal of confusion.

The second incident took place shortly after the "Baba" incident at work. Basically, my woman invited me to go out for dinner and meet her college friends. But what I think she may have failed to realise is that not only I am socially awkward, but also the King of Embarrassment. We had planned to go out for drinks and then have dinner at a fancy seafood restaurant that night. My awkwardness kicked in the minute we entered through the restaurant's doors. Part of the issue was that I felt uncomfortable among wealthy white people. However, my embarrassment occurred after we had found our table and placed our orders. Everyone was engaged in conversation, and I really hate small talk. I simply do not have the stomach for it. But the conversation was inexorably making its way towards me, and I had no choice but to take part in it. Otherwise, my continued silence at the table would defeat the purpose of the meal; everyone had come to meet me.

So, without giving it much thought, I rose to the challenge. I decided to keep the conversation flowing by sticking to the food topics raised 20 minutes earlier. I asked the following question and opened it to the group. Keep in mind that I was the only bloke among a group of eight females. So, although I looked like I was on an episode of the Bachelor, what happened next was unforgivable. Since we were in a seafood restaurant, I asked if anybody at the table had "ever had crabs before?"

As an African who grew up in a fishing village where fish was the only seafood on the menu, a crab was a luxury I had only seen on television. So my question was genuine. But the way I phrased it was the issue. I should have asked if anyone had ever *eaten* crabs not *had* crabs. *The former is a sea creature with a hard shell; the latter is a sexually transmitted disease (STD).* I vowed never to repeat that mistake again. Since then, I've been reading the dictionary every day and working hard to accept my oddity.

Despite this, I find myself making the same linguistic errors over and over again. Why is this happening to me? You might ask. I'm at a loss for words. Even my spelling is poor. I made a fool of myself once during a consultation when I questioned my doctor why there were so many leaflets and posters all around the office and parking lot that read "The Rapist Wanted."

I looked at my doctor in all seriousness and said, "Is

there anything you need to inform me or warn me about?"

"Like... is there a pervert out there, prowling around the community clinic... waiting to rape patients?"

Huh! What are you talking about? The doctor said

"No, I mean, the flyers and posters that you guys have at reception," I said. "It warns everyone coming here that they should be on the lookout for the rapist who is wanted by the police." Of course, I was expressing my honest and unfiltered interpretation of the content on the posters, but the doctor misconstrued me for making a rape joke, which I wasn't. When he saw I was serious, he burst out laughing, got up from his desk, and brought me out of his office to show me that the flyer said "Therapist Wanted" NOT "The rapist Wanted".

Before you laugh and criticise me for the millionth time, remember that it wasn't my fault this time. The leaflets and posters I saw outside had a space between the words "The" and "rapist." So, theoretically, it might be a typographical or printing error. I'm not shifting blame here, as you all know that the customer is always right. All I'm saying is that I believe there is a lesson to be learned here. For all of you office clerks out there, you should always have a proofreader go through your work before you click print. Following the encounter with the doctor, I decided to schedule an appointment with an optician on his advice, only to discover that I needed glasses. But that's completely irrelevant to what happened, isn't it?

What if the shoe was on the other foot? And this time, instead of being the customer, I was the one providing the service. Then look no further, for the following true-life experience will astound you. It involved a customer, and the blunder almost cost me my job. This time, the King of Embarrassment really screwed up, and I accept full blame. What happened was that a client passed away, and I had to contact their next of kin. After reviewing the guidelines and recommendations for dealing with consumers under such circumstances, I made sure my tone was extremely empathic. I asked the son a series of questions on the customer form, including his late father's private information and the date of death. Then I asked for the name and address of the "executor" of the deceased client. Now, in all my life, I had never seen this word used in this context, nor did I know how to pronounce it properly.

So again, I asked the grieving son, "Can you please give me the name and address of your father's executor?"

He was like, "I beg your pardon?"

I said, "E-x-e-c-u-t-o-r – the name and address."

He asked me what I meant by "executor." Without even giving it a second thought, I politely explained, "The name and address of the person who executed your father." I was referring to an executioner, an official who carries out the killing of a person who has been condemned to death. But then I paused and thought, that's an odd question to ask someone whose father just died. Hmmm! But it's in the guidance manual, so I might as well ask. So I repeated myself, but you could tell from my faint tone of voice that I was unconvinced.

"Who killed or murdered your father? We need you to tell us their name and find out where they live. " I asked the poor guy as if my boys and I were already planning to avenge the customer's death on his behalf, in some gang retaliation or something. I honestly didn't understand why the gentleman on the phone sounded so puzzled, especially as I was asking the right question and following the correct protocols. Now, as we both grew confused, I decided to put the gentleman on hold and ask one of my colleagues for help. That's when I found out what the word really meant.

An "executor" is someone who makes sure that things are done according to a deceased person's will. I came across as compunctious. Luckily, the gentleman understood that it was an honest mistake, and he didn't complain or take it any further. I think my friendly manner and the way I addressed him personally helped me out. Both my manager and teammates couldn't stop laughing afterwards; we were all in stitches. I guess I am no stranger to palm-to-face moments, am I? It felt like I was re-living the zip incident and wet daydreaming all over again. I am saying all of this just to show you that I am no angel. I am a human being, and I make mistakes like everyone else. I'm sure you, too, have done something crazy like that – or maybe not as bad, but still. My 9-5 was always full of surprises, to say the least. Despite the many ups and downs, we loved doing our job and helping members of the public. I liked the team I was assigned to, as it was very diverse and made up of people of African and Asian descent, as well as some white people. We had a lot of fun together, thanks to the forced camaraderie of office life.

I remember one incident where I invited some white guys from my team to a BAME event, as it was referred to back then. They had no clue what that was or what to expect, but they couldn't say no since they wanted to skive off work. Anyway, I couldn't stop laughing at their reaction the moment they realised that they were the only three white people in an auditorium packed with black people. They were a little fidgety and nervous. To calm them down and make them feel welcome, I kept cracking jokes and telling everyone that they were with me and that they had asked to come and see Wakanda. Everyone was so friendly towards them and they felt settled. Every now and then, during the programme, one of them would make eye contact with me, smile, and do the "Wakanda Forever" salute. To be honest, I didn't think much of the event at the time, but to those white guys it exceeded their

MICHAEL BANTU-KHOE

expectations. They approached me afterwards to say they had learnt so much, and their perspective on race and discrimination had changed.

I was so glad to hear them say that. However deep down I was itching to tell them that this was only just the beginning of the journey to becoming more actively anti-racist and active bystanders. I wanted to at least encourage them to not see this as a one-off thing or tick box exercise. To be an active allay, you need to continue to do your own homework when it comes to gaining an insight into the concerns or lived experiences of black and brown people. This ongoing learning can help you understand the impact of racism and can often act as a catalyst for change. "Now, no one can do this work for you." That's what I further said to them. "It's something that has to come from within you." As much as you can lead a horse to water, you can't make it drink. "You have to decide for yourself whether you want to be anti-racist or not." The choice is yours. "

Looking back, I somehow have some regrets because if I knew beforehand that attending this event would have such an impact on my white colleagues who attended with me, I may as well have extended the invitation to the entire office staff. I think they would have benefited from the training because not long before that, myself and another Asian colleague, on separate incidents, got racial discriminated against right at our workplace. I will not repeat what was said to my fellow Asian colleague because that is not my story to tell, but I will share with you what was said to me. And before I do that, I just want to say for the record, like most black people, I've experienced more cutthroat and heart-breaking forms of racism, but honestly speaking, the one racial incident I seem incapable of moving past is this one that took place at my place of work. The experience seems to sting the most, and I don't know why.

The workplace incident was more subtle and covert. I mean, tell me, what do you do when you're a newbie and a white colleague charged with training you stands up to crack a joke at your expense and says to her friends, "Hey guys, look, I've got my own black slave working for me!"? Well, in my case, you try hard to convince yourself that you haven't heard what you just heard. That happened to me in the first few weeks of

MICHAEL BANTU-KHOE

starting my job. What's even worse was that my manager, who also happened to be white, saw everything in real-time, yet her immediate reaction was to rush towards me to insist that my colleague didn't mean it like that. I mean, what kind of nonsense is that? How could that be interpreted as anything other than offensive?

I was utterly bamboozled. I couldn't even respond to what was happening. I stayed dead silent during the incident and gave a fake, simpering smile. I never once complained, filed a grievance, or even voiced my opinion until now. As someone with a calm temperament, I couldn't bring myself to call out racism when it happened to me. My mind was somewhere else, far away, and I was focused more on making a good impression, keeping my job, and not causing any trouble. I was so fixated on keeping this 'good-guy' persona that I didn't fully register what was going on.

I sometimes feel that I have to be extra polite in the company of Caucasian managers, smile and look extra happy, and even appear to be more accommodating and welcoming to make them feel at ease. In her book, The

Loudest Duck: Moving Beyond Diversity while Embracing Differences to Achieve Success at Work, Laura Liswood articulates this with an anecdote about a mouse and an elephant. She says to imagine a room containing these two animals. If you're the elephant in the room, how much do you need to know about the mouse to survive? Not much. Your massive foot can trample the mouse with one accidental step. Yet, if you are the mouse in the room, how much do you need to know about the elephant? Just about everything—you need to predict its movements, know its habits, anticipate its rituals. The elephant knows almost nothing about the mouse, but the mouse survives by knowing everything about the elephant. Herein lies the dynamic between the dominant and non-dominant groups in the workplace.

In the workplace, there are norms and ways of being that come naturally to the dominant group. Yet, for a team to truly thrive, these elephants must become aware that their experiences aren't everyone's reality. They must shift their perspective to see how much and how well mice can contribute, and foster an environment where the mice, giraffes, lions, antelopes, and slippery dicks can all bring their unique skills and perspectives to the table. For your own information, and by the way, feel free to look it up, a "slippery dick" is a type of fish, so shame on you if you thought of something else.

And speaking of fish, Albert Einstein is often credited with this wonderful quote, but it may actually have come from a variety of different sources. The quote is quite fitting given its subject matter and how it relates to managing a diverse workforce. It says, and I am paraphrasing, "If you judge a fish by its ability to climb a tree, it will live its whole life believing that it is stupid." So therein lies another valuable lesson in that everyone has something they are good at and can bring to the table.

In my department, about 200-300 of us were split across the entire building floors. Most teams had a mixture of people from different walks of life and backgrounds. I noticed, however, that all the line managers were white, and there was not a single black or Asian manager. You couldn't make this stuff up, people; it was as clear as day. It was very apparent that many black and Asian people occupied the lowest grades, and all had white managers.

I sat next to another African who had worked for the department for almost 20 years and was still at the same low level or grade. I asked her respectfully whether she had ever considered promotion or applied for a higher grade. She said that she was interested, but after numerous failed attempts, she reached a point where she felt helpless and didn't see the point in trying anymore. I was taken aback by her comments, but the more I looked around, the more it made sense. There were a lot of black co-workers like her in the same predicament. When I saw her frown in sadness, it reminded me of the look my mum would give me when we had nothing to live on. I was prepared to fight this tooth and nail. If not for me, let me do it for other black co-workers who, like her, felt powerless. As a result, I decided to take the initiative and volunteer for various jobs and responsibilities, such as delivering presentations and conducting surveys. I became aware of the mentoring programmes, and after enrolling in them and participating for a few months, I gained a great deal of knowledge.

MICHAEL BANTU-KHOE

My mentors' one-on-one mentoring encouraged me to improve and acquire much more confidence. I joined networks and met others who shared my interests. I also searched for opportunities such as seminars that taught staff how to write resumes and demonstrate job competencies. I even went through interview training and requested feedback on any unsuccessful job interviews. As a result, I was quite optimistic and upbeat about the future, and I felt like I was making progress. And it was at that moment that I was fortunate enough to cross paths with someone who offered me words of encouragement that fuelled my success and pushed me to achieve things I had previously considered impossible.

That person was none other than Jacky Wright. I wasn't surprised when I found out later that she was included in a publication by Powerful Media presenting Britain's 10 Most Influential Black People list from African, African-Caribbean, and African American backgrounds. Jacky Wright was ranked in the number one spot on the UK Powerlist 2022 on October 14, 2021. Marcus Rashford, the England footballer and campaigner, came in second place.

MICHAEL BANTU-KHOE

I'll tell you how someone completely unrelated to her and as insignificant as myself ended up on Jacky's radar. Every time I got a new job, the first thing I did was scan the organisation chart to see whether anybody looked like me. This black lady, whom I'd never seen before, was the first and only one I'd seen at the senior level. When I initially got promoted and joined her department, I was surprised to learn that she was on her way out. She was leaving the organisation to go work for a giant technological firm in America.

I sent her a beautifully crafted email moments before the end of her one-month notice, wishing her the best in her future endeavours I also didn't shy away from expressing how heartbroken I was that she was leaving her post. I told her the whole thing. Since entering the organisation, I have seldom seen individuals like me in managerial or senior positions. When you don't see yourself reflected back like that as a young black person, it conveys the message that you don't matter or that you're not good enough because of your skin colour. She responded to my email, which surprised me. She urged me to persevere and make myself available.

MICHAEL BANTU-KHOE

Sooner or later, she said, you will be recognised for your talents.

I took her words to heart and ran with them, shining brightly. I soon came to realise why she said I should persevere. You know, perseverance is closely tied to resilience. To persevere in the face of adversity and keep working toward one's goals, in particular when the odds are stacked against you, requires both resilience and perseverance. How often do you hear people say, "Pressure makes diamonds"? Nevertheless, despite this fact, I am well aware that not all of us possess the resilience necessary to cope with the mentally and emotionally draining stress as well as the challenges that come along with being subjected to discrimination in the workplace.

By extending out and allowing my abilities and talents to flourish in an environment that was predominantly a white-led sector, I stuck out like a sore thumb. My passion and drive were the things that they hated the most. I could see in their eyes that they thought I was out to take their jobs. Because I posed a danger to their so-called white privilege, it was imperative that I be reprimanded and silenced in order to maintain their status quo. It's difficult to express that sensation to someone who has never been in that situation. With no disrespect to the visually impaired, articulating the challenges and difficulties of being the lone black person in a room is akin to describing the many shades of green to someone who is colourblind, in the hope that they fully understand.

One such example that bears witness to this is when I found myself in a boardroom meeting at work with around 30 other individuals, all of whom were white. I was the only black person there. This wasn't your typical meeting, or so I thought. We were all there to make decisions about the department's future goals and to explore ways of putting such decisions into action for the whole department. I hardly made a contribution since every follow-up remark after I spoke was either undercut, overlocked, or completely disregarded the issues that I had brought up in the discussion. Now, I'm not arguing that I felt excluded just for those reasons, or that my ideas and perspectives are immune to criticism. That's not the point I'm trying to make at all.

MICHAEL BANTU-KHOE

All I'm saying is that, being the only black person in the office, I wasn't taken as seriously as my other co-workers. I recognised a pattern of behaviour in which whenever I attempted to speak out or make a point, it seemed like I was overstepping my bounds. In fact, during the discussion, one of the managers sitting next to me kept on interrupting me. Basically, he was talking over me as I attempted to make a point, which was really impolite in my opinion. Unfortunately, no one came to my defence, not even the chairman of that meeting. You know things are bad when no one wants to speak up for you and urge their colleague to be respectful and let me complete my case.

Despite this, the moment that truly seemed like salt being rubbed into the wound was when, in one of his interruptions, he stopped to ask me whether I was taking notes on the topic. My pen and paper were in plain sight, and he could tell that I'd been taking notes during the discussion. But it was the manner in which he asked me that was so subtle and rubbed me the wrong way. As if to say, we don't want to hear what you have to say; you're simply here to take notes.

MICHAEL BANTU-KHOE

The more we had these sorts of meetings, the quieter and quieter I got at them. I was obviously disregarded and undervalued. I gradually felt a suffocating pressure that discouraged me from bringing my whole self to work. My white co-workers seemed to be the complete antithesis of who I was. The culture of the organisation was very restrictive for people of African descent. Turning up to work every day and trying hard to fit in felt like trying to get a giraffe to live in a house built for a dog. I mean that there were times when I attempted to blend in by sounding white and playing along with everyone else by laughing at every joke and conforming to their expectations of how I should act. But it only appeared to work for a short time. Until one of them, at an after-work party, eventually feels comfortable enough to say to you, "You know what I like about you, Michael?" I like that you are different from other black people! You are one of the good ones. "

It's difficult to shrug off that comment and consider it as a praise when it's actually an insult to both myself and people of colour. In some ways, I'm delighted he told me that. It gave me with a swift reality check on where

I stood as a black co-worker. I undoubtedly felt like an outsider who did not belong in that group.

Despite the antagonism at work, I made the most of my time spent travelling to work by listening to podcasts and radio shows. One day, on The Breakfast Club radio show, I came across an interview with Kanye West, who was outlining Jay-Z's business ethos. "Jay, know how to move in a room full of vultures," Kanye said. That certainly piqued my interest. Kanye then said that being likeable can sometimes work in your favour by persuading a large audience to support you or even getting your foot in the door in white working-class America.

As I listened, I had to admit that I agreed with him while also disagreeing with myself. The truth is, I strived to be like Jay-Z, and trust me, it doesn't always pan out the way you'd expect. My whole life, I've been the type of person who could tolerate almost anything that was thrown my way. In the beginning, when it came to working for and with white people, I was, at times, your typical yes man; a people pleaser. I've always made sacrifices for others because of the way I was raised. I genuinely give so much thought to other people's sentiments that I nearly always forget about my own. It's the classic middle child syndrome.

In all essence, work had almost become a nuisance for me. Being the lone black worker at meetings and gatherings made me anxious. As soon as I walked into these rooms, I realised I didn't have to say anything. People had already formed the notion that I was the tokenised black person, a checkbox that the organisation needed to check in order to seem credible to outsiders.

At work, I often found myself being a silent spectator in most of these white-dominated meetings I was invited to. Then, when I tried to change roles and move up the ladder, I was denied several times. It's no wonder you often hear people say most businesses, organisations and major corporations can be likened to a mountain: the higher you go, the whiter it gets. For some black people, climbing the career ladder is not as straightforward as it is for our white counterparts. Ours is more like a zigzag whereby you almost certainly have to jump between organisations to progress in your career and move up the ladder.

The glass ceiling is very much a reality. For all we know, black and brown people have been fighting for recognition at the highest levels of society and business for a good number of years. However, they are still up against an invisible, systemic barrier that prevents them from entering certain spaces, such as decision rooms. where critical decisions concerning their communities are made without their input, participation, or agreement.

A recent conversation on social media captured the essence of this problem to the letter. We've all seen images which are still very much fresh in our memories; of H&M's allegedly racist ad showcasing a black child wearing the "Coolest Monkey in the Jungle" outfit. Thankfully, following a public protest, that ad was pulled down. And how about the controversy over the Gucci brand's $890 turtleneck sweater, which included a bright red lip as a cut-out for the mouth and was criticised for resembling blackface? Indeed, some of these racial blind spots on the part of these major corporations are rather inexcusable and should not be tolerated.

Now, here is another one that almost broke the internet. Do you recall this commercial advertisement for Intel, which depicts a white manager/boss standing amid six black guys who are bowing down their heads? Despite the fact that they intended to "convey the performance capabilities of Intel Processors through the visual metaphor of a sprinter," the end result was something quite different. Their ad selection was blatantly racist in my opinion. This goes to show you how much we need black and brown individuals in positions of power to call or stymie discriminatory adverts before they are broadcast to the general public.

And this does not only help with racism, but according to a business article that was published on the website entrepreneur.com, when everyone on a team thinks the same way, there is little space for invention, creating a stifling environment for inventing the next great thing. People from all walks of life, on the other hand, perceive the world from a wider perspective and provide distinct intellectual capital to the organisations for which they work.

Listening to the perspectives of people with different experiences leads to more in-depth brainstorming sessions, which promote outside-the-box thinking and higher levels of creativity in today's firms. These sessions may provide a concept or product that can assist a business in differentiating itself from its competitors and become more successful.

Furthermore, diversified thinking leads to greater customer satisfaction. It is difficult to serve the end user if a company's decision-making team does not contain individuals who can connect to that customer. A diverse staff is more likely to relate to the goals, needs, and pain points of a certain audience, offering more opportunity to connect with consumers. A varied workforce also opens up the possibility of reaching new populations in ways that would not have been possible with a homogeneous group at the helm. Finally, increased levels of diversity may boost customer volume and satisfaction, which increases profitability. The crux of the matter is that, in order to combat, we urgently need more black individuals and diverse groups in positions of authority. It's not fair to keep us out of the decision-making process in these places. But at the same time, when we do manage to grab a seat at the table, it is often just one or two of us black folks sitting in the middle of a bunch of white males.

And worse still, even at that, we tend to take on the role of spectators rather than participants the majority of the time. And as a direct consequence of this, a great number of businesses make appallingly, or rather dreadful, prejudiced judgments on the advertising campaigns they run because there is a lack of diversity and representation in the rooms where these decisions are made. This contemporary lack of inclusion issue is prominent not just in the commercial sector, but it is also replicated in all of the many parts of society. So, if we want to solve this problem, we need to make significant changes as soon as possible.

Perhaps the best place to begin with is by looking intently at an unlikely source, highly recommended by my mother, by the way. Being a Christian, I often look to the Bible for answers to life's core issues. As a result, when it comes to discrimination and bigotry, I strive to get the most out of my reading from the Holy Book. One of my favourite biblical passages that openly discusses this is found in Acts 6:1-3.

It portrays the story of discrimination that may have caused schism in the newly established Christian church. When food was distributed to destitute widows, Greek-speaking widows were overlooked as compared to the Hebrew-speaking widows (prejudices over language may have been a factor). The apostles quickly rectified the matter by appointing qualified men to handle the food distribution. All these spiritually qualified men had Greek names, which may have made them more acceptable to the offended widows. This was a well-thought-out and kind consideration.

Therefore, the lesson that I gleaned from that is that in order for us to achieve diversity and equality, we need to prioritise representation while at the same time being proactive and not be afraid to stump out any tendencies or traits of bigotry that exist in all levels of society.

MICHAEL BANTU-KHOE

DECOLONISING

THE

WORKPLACE

MICHAEL BANTU-KHOE

On May 25, 2020, we all saw the heinous murder of a 46-year-old man, George Floyd, while he was in the custody of Minneapolis, Minnesota, police. The sight of Derek Chauvin, a former police officer and convicted murderer, knelling on George Floyd's neck for nine minutes and 29 seconds, asphyxiating him. When you consider all of these factors, including

MICHAEL BANTU-KHOE

Floyd's repeated pleas of "I can't breathe," and hearing him calling out to his deceased mother in that situation, it is both excruciatingly painful and heartbreaking to see.

Soon after George Floyd's brutal execution, many people all over the world felt the need to acknowledge that racism and brutality against Black people are still part of the contemporary world rather than being a mere thing of the past. When I say, "many people," what I am really referring to is a population that is mostly white. Tragically, it has taken yet another horrible, sadistic, and very public killing of another Black man to prick the conscience of many people and make them realise that racism is, in fact, a serious problem around the world.

Since that realisation, a lot of institutions all over the world have jolted in solidarity, issuing a number of statements condemning racism and expressing support for the Black communities. If you've been following along with the latest HR trends, you'll have noticed that the transformation to a more inclusive and ethical workplace is gaining momentum. In fact, a lot of workplaces are recognising the need to remove colonial ideologies and practices that are embedded into the structure of their organisations. If your company is one of them, I genuinely applaud you! However, if that doesn't describe your current situation, maybe it's time for you to consider making some changes. After all, having a toxic work environment can be detrimental to your health and performance.

The truth of the matter is, racism and other forms of discrimination are pervasive in the workplace. They exist both consciously and unconsciously and it takes a lot of work to dismantle them. As a result, there is a need for organisations to focus their attention and efforts on deconstructing ideologies and practises that perpetuate racism in the workplace. This means addressing unconscious biases as well as creating policies that will improve representation across all levels of employment within an organisation.

In this Chapter I'll give you an introduction on how to decolonise the workplace, so your organisation becomes more inclusive and ethical. Before I proceed, allow me to first define what I mean by "decolonisation." Decolonisation is the process of shedding colonial ideologies and practices that are embedded into the structure of organisations. It involves acknowledging the impact of colonisation and understanding how this has shaped today's workplace culture. The goal is to cultivate an environment that is welcoming of all perspectives and values, and in which everyone has the opportunity to thrive.

Colonialism is about white supremacy, so it's no surprise that it has negatively affected people of colour, women, and other minority groups. Decolonising is not an act of charity, it's an ethical and moral responsibility. You can't just sit there and expect things to change on their own. Rather, it's a continuous effort that every individual is responsible for. By decolonising the workplace, you are acknowledging the voices and experiences of people who have been historically silenced or excluded. It is not merely a matter of changing the physical space, it's about challenging the culture and assumptions that exist in your organisation.

A decolonised workplace offers a space that listens and respects the experiences of employees from all backgrounds. There is a strong emphasis on equal treatment and empowerment for all employees. There is a sense of community and belonging that permeates all levels of the organisation, making it a desirable place to work. Decolonisation is not about creating separate spaces, but instead creating space for everyone. An inclusive and decolonised workplace offers the same opportunities for everyone. There are clear expectations, guidelines, and policies in place that ensure that everyone is treated respectfully.

If your workplace is already toxic, you may be thinking it's too late to do anything about it. But don't give up! It's never too late to try and affect change. If your company is already toxic, it may be because you've never had the opportunity to decolonise it. There are many simple ways you can start to rebuild a toxic workplace. A great place to start is by decolonising HR practices and policies.

One of the major problems with many modern workplaces is the lack of racial and ethnic diversity. This can be traced back to the colonial ideologies and practices that are still present in many organisations.

MICHAEL BANTU-KHOE

For example, some companies may be using colonial language in their policies or measuring employees based on the imperial system. This type of language and practices are extremely exclusionary, so you could start by replacing them with terms that are more inclusive and sensitive to minorities. You could also implement new policies that promote inclusion and equality. For example, you could create a policy that requires managers to rotate positions to ensure that everyone is getting an opportunity to advance and develop their skills. You could also implement an unconscious bias training that educates your employees on how stereotypes and biases impact their judgements.

Unconscious biases are not limited to racial discrimination—they also include prejudice towards other groups such as gender, sexual orientation or even social class. It's important to recognise that everyone has these biases—even the most progressive of us—and that it's possible for the effects of unconscious bias to lead us astray from our goals if we don't address them properly in the workplace environment. To counter act this negative unconscious bias, we therefore need to implement policies that improve representation. Such as having a clear and transparent policy on diversity and inclusion, equal opportunity, bullying and harassment and Race discrimination etc.

Another critical part is to promote in your organisation an open and honest dialogue about racism. It is important that you encourage your employees to talk about their experiences of racism at work, especially if they have never felt comfortable doing so in the past. This can be done through setting up regular meetings and safe havens where people who have experienced racism are given time to speak about their experiences and provide feedback on how it has affected them.

However, as with everything else, there is a strong need to exercise caution. Although it may seem like common sense, not everyone feels comfortable sharing all of their feelings or thoughts with others—especially if they feel as though they will be judged for doing so. However, allowing people to express themselves openly and honestly will help encourage an environment where everyone feels safe enough to share these types of things without feeling as though they might get in trouble for doing so.

MICHAEL BANTU-KHOE

The bottom line is, every employee should feel they have the right to speak up and share their experiences, even if that means they're speaking out against their own colleagues. Encourage honesty and openness among your staff by providing them with a platform to do so. Employees who feel comfortable talking about their experiences will be able to bring their whole selves into the workplace, leading to better collaboration and more productive discussions on how best to tackle incidents of racism. If you want your company culture to reflect the values of decolonisation, apply the above suggestions and, trust me, give it time and you'll thank me later.

Decolonising the office requires us to focus on the HR (human resources) department. HR departments play an important role in mitigating racial tensions in the workplace. HR employees must be educated on how to appropriately handle discrimination at work. Employees may feel more comfortable if an HR department establishes a working environment in which they can express their thoughts. They can also help employees who are experiencing racism understand their rights and responsibilities as an employee, or even help you understand your own views on race if you find yourself in a situation where you need to talk about it with another person at work or outside of work.

While the HR department is working to create a more inclusive workplace, it's important to remember that people of colour, and other groups are often hesitant to call out racism. You might think this is because these things don't exist in your workplace—but that's probably not the case. When someone is being discriminated against or harassed based on their identity, they often feel like they won't be taken seriously by management. As a result, they might not speak up when they experience discrimination.

It's important for all employees in an organisation to feel comfortable calling out racism, and other forms of discrimination. If you want to create an inclusive culture at work where everyone feels safe doing so, there are several steps you can take. The first one is to give employees the tools they need to speak out about harassment; this might include training on how best to handle complaints so that everyone feels comfortable reporting them quickly when necessary. The second point is making sure managers know there is zero tolerance for any form of discrimination whatsoever.

Another fundamental issue to address is recruiting, namely, how to deal with biassed hiring practices. This is because racial and/or implicit bias is embedded deep in the recruitment and selection process and that prejudice is clouding the screening of qualified candidates. To decolonise the hiring process, we need to adopt a diverse interview panel. Create recruiting and hiring teams with a diverse range of experiences and backgrounds. Make diversity training mandatory for anybody who is engaged in the process of hiring or recruiting new employees.

If circumstances allow, Include, if possible, a question on the application form for the applicant to choose whether or not they would want to be interviewed by a diverse panel. As someone who has been an interviewee before, I can say with absolute certainty that having a diverse panel helps me feel more at ease. Through the years of leading recruiting efforts, I've seen a number of significant issues, and I believe that my suggestion will help alleviate one of the following issues.

It is no secret that some white managers or employers would rather appoint or promote people who look like them than select talented and smart people from different races or backgrounds. When it comes to race, it is almost as though the mere presence of a black person causes them to experience some kind of fear and anxiety. Without a doubt, this behaviour or norm must be eliminated in order for the workplace to become decolonized.

These days many businesses focus on recruitment as a way to attempt to increase diversity in the workforce or build credibility with stakeholders. It can also be part of a broader strategy to ensure the workforce is skilled in areas that will help the business grow and succeed in the future. However, although this may all seem fantastic, it may turn out to be a double-edged sword. HR and hiring managers need to be alert to this potential red flag. And that red flag for me is token hiring, sometimes referred to as "tokenism," which is usually associated with discrimination against groups with whom the employer does not traditionally associate themselves. In my opinion, I am against the practice of hiring token minorities in an effort to appear diverse or inclusive.

I've heard some people vouch that, in some cases, there may be good reasons to hire a token minority employee. For instance, exclusively hiring individuals with local knowledge in a specific niche field or profession. And that may be true. However, for the majority of companies, I do want to caution recruiters to bear this in mind. That, when you employ someone for any position or role, it shouldn't be solely based on the colour of their skin but rather on their good merits. I do stand to be corrected, but in my opinion, tokenism should always be avoided at all costs if you want to build a diverse and inclusive workplace culture.

I know it's possible that the following example would seem to contradict everything else I've stated about tokenism up to this point, but please give me a chance to explain myself before passing judgement. A couple of years back, I once worked for an organisation where I was part of the Race Working Group, responsible for supporting ethnic minority groups to have a voice in the majority white-led organisation. Being continually active in that group came with its own challenges, as you would expect, and one of them was figuring out how to keep my sanity when I kept on hearing some of the sanitised appeals and lip-service pledges from senior executives regarding dealing with racism at work.

In all honesty, it was quite difficult for me, as a black man, to get excited about anything having to do with racism at work. Given the regularity with which this happens, I couldn't help but wonder: are these folks telling the truth, or are they simply saying it because it's the current trend to do so? I was always concerned for us black and brown people working there because every hurried announcement felt like, once again, they were attempting to pull the wool over our eyes and make this a company tick box exercise.

After giving what these top senior executives had to say such careful consideration, I constantly found myself at odds with some of the choices and actions involving racial issues at work. I felt that some decisions were incompatible with my values and beliefs. For instance, if you claim to care deeply about the plight of black people in your organisation and that you want to give them a voice and help them gain the skills they need to advance in their careers, why would you then go about and appoint or promote a privileged white person to become their Race Champion and Executive Committee lead? Why promote a white person to such a high-level position while also making them the "Face of the Race campaign," to which every black colleague is expected to flock in order to escape workplace bigotry? What message are you sending to the rest of your black employees in your organisation? Do they themselves need a white saviour? I have to confess that being a part of that Race working Group and at the same time being forced to directly answer to someone who has never been subjected to racism in their whole life was a very strange experience for me.

My feelings on the matter were quite divided because I couldn't fathom why the organisation would choose to put a white person in charge of a large group of individuals who have been marginalised and are most likely to encounter racism on a day-to-day basis. What kind of loopholes do they have that allow them to get away with this? Being a member of that group made me feel really ashamed since almost all of the people who held leadership positions on the executive committee and in charge of race relations were white. Also, I want to make it clear that I am not intending to make any disparaging remarks about those particular white folks. I have no doubt that the majority of them are kind and decent human beings, and maybe even wonderful allies.

However, the fact remains that, while you may sympathise with the black struggle, they have no idea what it's like to be black—no matter how much research they do or how hard they try, they'll never understand it on an intellectual level. So how can we justify that to the younger black generation of workers and convince them that somebody who looks like their oppressor has their best interests at heart? That is the question for which I have difficulty finding an answer.

In my view, the situation may be remedied by paying careful attention to the valuable lesson included in the following analogy. See, if the fight for equality in the workplace were a female group called Destiny's Child, the ally wouldn't be the lead singer, Beyonce, or the second vocalist, Kelly Rowland. Instead, the ally in this case would be Michell Williams, and I don't mean any disrespect to you, Michelle; your voice is incredible, and you're still an important member of the group. But that's the point I am making here. We're happy to have white allies help us fight and stand for the oppressed, but to have you at the forefront leading our movements is nothing but disrespectful, I'm afraid.

Many businesses and organizations have embraced diversity hiring practices, but they have yet to address the problem of racism in their own offices. If they hope to win the respect of customers and employees of colour—as well as maintain their own reputations— they should address internal issues of racism head-on. And that includes how to address internal grievances raised by employees inside your organisation.

There are certain policies, processes, and behaviours that may allow racism to seep in through and eventually tarnish your company's reputation. When handling certain internal incidents of racism, it may be helpful if you could white folks not to jump ahead and volunteer as decision makers or judges unless they are well-versed or knowledgeable about the topic of racism. I am not saying you should exclude yourself from the process altogether; however, at least know your privilege and where you stand. The truth is, for some of you it is your racial blind spots and bias towards people of colour that have become the root of the problem.

And by racial blind spot, I am referring to an area of life where you have little to no experience with people of a certain race. As an example, if you are white and grew up in the suburbs without any black friends or neighbours until college, then that would be your racial blind spot. If someone who grew up in Harlem were to ask this person if they had ever been discriminated against by police officers before—and the answer was "no"—then that too would be their racial blind spot.

The importance of identifying these blind spots lies within their ability to influence our decision-making processes; research has shown that when we're unaware of our own biases (or lack thereof), we'll make decisions based on those unconscious assumptions rather than basing them on facts and evidence available at hand! This can lead us down problematic paths like hiring more white people for jobs over equally qualified candidates from other ethnic groups due simply because "they look like me."

There are many different ways to identify your racial blind spots. One way is by talking with someone who has experienced racism first-hand and listening intently while they share their story; another method involves asking friends or colleagues what they think about race-related topics and listening nonjudgmentally when they respond (even if it's hard not to get defensive). If this doesn't work, then try doing some research online—but beware of becoming overwhelmed!

Now circling back around to the grievance process. You know who's got it the hardest? The people who have to try and explain, again and again their race-related trauma to a clueless white person who has never been subjected to racism in their life but rather has to somehow impartially pass or render judgement on the grievance case.

I'm not talking about the person who is experiencing the pain of racism—I'm talking about the person trying to help that white judge understand why that pain is happening. I've seen it first-hand: when you're already dealing with racial trauma… and someone else wants you to educate them on what racism is? That's just adding insult to injury. I personally found that to be even more detrimental to one's mental health than the other.

The grievance process is meant to provide a safe space for people who have experienced discrimination, harassment, or other forms of mistreatment. But many persons of colour have found that when the accused racist offender is of a senior background, executive level, or somebody deemed important in the company, it can be challenging to get justice for what happened to them.

A lot of times, human resource department or HR will ask another executive manager or someone in the same circle to handle the grievance complaint and make a final decision. But what if the very senior manager HR selects has some kind of connection with the alleged offender? For example, suppose they often hang out on weekends or play golf together and now one of them is asked to serve as a judge in a grievance case in which their other golfing buddy is being accused of being racist by a subordinate colleague? How would this judge rule? In my considered opinion, this is where organizations and businesses should pay more than usual attention and put precautions into place in order to stop incidents like this from ever occurring again!

I have encountered multiple occurrences similar to the hypothetical one mentioned above from different departments and establishments outside of work. I'm afraid that for most of these cases, the ending more often than not turns out to favour the accused perpetrator, and the episode of racial abuse is subsequently brushed under the rug or labelled as a learning lesson for those involved. And that's often one of the underlying problems that deter us from raising grievances and complaints as black and brown people.

Raising a grievance or complaint does not mean that we are seeking revenge but rather an acknowledgment of wrongdoing, an apology, and some form of amends so as to move forward with our lives. The fact that these perpetrators feel emboldened after experiencing these shady or questionable internal grievance wins is not a coincidence. It's the result of how HR handles these cases. Usually, the complainant gets hit with a grievance outcome from human resource (HR) that states something along the lines of, "while your grievance case was unsuccessful, we've made a few recommendations to the other party to undergo an internal Race training workshop event or program." They are, however, under no obligation to show up for the event in question. And forget about human resource (HR) following up to see whether that particular manager had attended such a course or not.

The time has come for HR to stop making excuses and allow perpetrators to hide behind their executive privileges, encouraging them to continue with their racist tendencies and inflicting pain on their next black or brown targets. The idea that executives can get away with any kind of behaviour because of their titles is just wrong. We have the right to be protected from discrimination, harassment, and other forms of abuse by our employers—and those who are guilty should be punished accordingly. Therefore, HR needs to stop enabling this behaviour by holding executives accountable for their actions and making sure they understand that there will be consequences if they continue to discriminate against others based on race or ethnicity.

If you're reading this, I'm going to assume that you want to make your workplace a more inclusive and equal place. It's a difficult goal, but it's one that is achievable with the right approach. I'm sure that some of the above strategies will be met with resistance. This is why it is so critical to engage in open and honest conversation about racism and other forms of discrimination in the workplace. The more we talk about these issues, the more likely it is that we can solve them together and decolonise the workplace.

MICHAEL BANTU-KHOE

THE ROOTS

OF DISCORD

MICHAEL BANTU-KHOE

The fact that we are nearing the end of this book makes me feel pretty downtrodden and melancholy. But before we say our most heart-breaking goodbyes, I just want to come out and say that I am so glad that I decided to go on this adventure. Even more thrilling is the fact that you were able to come along for the ride, and I hope that you both laughed and learned with me along the way. This has undoubtedly been a dream

MICHAEL BANTU-KHOE

come true, especially for this middle-born, African child who grappled with an "identity crisis" as a result of growing up in a large family of twelve. I believe it's fair to say that I learned to fend for myself even when I got lost in the sibling shuffle. And who knows, if I hadn't gone through the training, how else would I have dealt with some of life's thorniest issues that eventually came my way? How else could I have learned to deal with issues related to my mental health and discrimination if I hadn't been humbled?

In all candour, I am of the opinion that comedy and tragedy are two sides of the same coin. I hope you found it engaging and fascinating, because some portions of my book are laugh-out-loud amusing, providing a relevant juxtaposition with the anguish of my job experiences before suddenly sinking into seriousness. If anything, it exemplifies how soul-sapping racism can be, as well as how it can transform an upbeat or jovial young man into an agitated one. Thus, living one's life in the shadows, which to me, is akin to living in an air-conditioned hell.

MICHAEL BANTU-KHOE

Do you want to hear something else that's completely off the wall? For as long as I can remember, one of my goals has been to come up with a comprehensive book with a rich title, one that has broad-based perspectives or dimensions of meaning. However, getting there wasn't exactly a walk in the park! The thought process itself left me mentally fragile because I had to do some self-reflection on my life experiences. Therefore, the idea for the title of this book sprang from one of my childhood's painful memories.

When I was younger, our parents taught us to believe in heaven and hell. The concept of a flaming inferno has always terrified me. As a youngster, I was often labelled as a bad kid. Some of the grownups used the word "bad" to describe my actions or myself. So, naturally, when I was taught that bad people eventually go to hell, I was traumatised. I've always internalised that feeling of being stuck in a place of torment for eternity, the underworld, where all evil or bad people go to when they die.

My parents were Roman Catholics at the time, and so to inculcate in us the concept of good and evil, they hung a cheap replica painting by Pieter Huys called The Last Judgement on the wall, which purported to portray life after death. It depicted good people ascending to heaven and becoming angels, while wicked people plummeted into the underworld and were tormented for eternity in a blazing fire. With my eyes closed, I could recall every detail of that artwork and, more or less, the emotion it evoked in me.

Those feelings horrified me as a child, and it wasn't until recently, in my late twenties, that I stopped having nightmares of being tormented by flames in hell. I used to wake up screaming in the middle of the night, about how I was being hurled into some kind of fiery realm. Needless to say, I made every effort not to transgress or sin out of sheer terror of being sent into hell. A combination of weekly therapy sessions and regular Bible study helped me conquer that phobia. I was very keen to explore the very idea of hellfire in the afterlife. After doing extensive research and studying every piece of evidence I could find on the issue, I turned to the Bible to see what it had to say about the genesis of hellfire. I learnt the correct Biblical understanding of the meaning of hell and its usage in the Holy Writings.

It was a relief to learn that the word "hell" as used in the Bible is not a place of fiery torment but rather the same word is used interchangeably with a Greek word, "Hades," which translates as "man's common grave." The evidence from the Bible made complete and total sense. How the misconception first began and made its way to the popular mainstream is another conversation for another day. The moral of the story is that true faith is not blind, and it is built on facts and real evidence. That minute discovery was the key to unlocking many questionable doors in my mind.

There are numerous negative things, including false opinions of oneself, that are deeply engrained in our minds and impact us when we become adults. When I was a kid, I was told that if you saw a crimson sky at sunset, it was a sign that wicked people were burning in the flames of hell. This was something that I believed to be true. Not only was it a harrowing experience, but it also stopped me, for a number of years, from enjoying the lovely, breath-taking, picturesque sights around me. I've reached the point in my life when all I crave is to live in a city with polluted skies. I am thrilled that my quest for self-discovery liberated me mentally from the cage of my own fears and worries. Sometimes we need to take dramatic measures to unshackle ourselves from the psychological bonds of religious dogma, mind control, and other people's perceptions of us.

Today, I believe that spending one's life in an air-conditioned hell can be characterised as attempting to find comfort in perpetual discomfort. As a mental health advocate, I know what it's like to suffer in silence and have my mental health condition misunderstood by others. If you have severe depression, anxiety, or any other debilitating medical condition, I pray and hope that somewhere in this book I've inspired you to continue pushing through the discomfort. I emphasise the word "continue" because sometimes our circumstances may or may not change, and that's okay. Learning to accept one's own reality is indeed a true sign of character strength. One that would serve you well in life if you took each day as it came.

I also believe that from a racial, economic, spiritual, and even political standpoint, living your life in an air-conditioned hell can refer to you being courageous and steadfast, and not losing hope in the face of obstacles, persecutions, trials, or even temptations. This is something that I find to be the case. Even in the office, where you are sometimes required to exist or operate in an atmosphere that is unfavourable, unfriendly, and maybe even toxic. To achieve success despite the fact that the odds are stacked against you, you will need a significant amount of courage. That, to me, epitomises living in an air-conditioned hell.

The same logic may be applied to those of us who are now enduring the ravages of the COVID-19 epidemic. It's been widely reported that millions of families from around the world have been impacted by this dreadful virus in some shape or form. My heart goes out to you all who have lost loved ones during these difficult times. Coping with grief and loss can be really hard because the pain never really goes away completely. And, to be honest, it can take a long time to begin the process of healing or even to begin picking up the pieces and moving on with life.

I know how difficult that can be because, whilst writing and finalising this book, I sadly lost my father during the COVID-19 pandemic. It was without a doubt the worst day of my life when it occurred. What's more, I couldn't even attend his funeral in Botswana due to all the travel restrictions. I was the only one from overseas who couldn't make it. It aches my heart to know that I couldn't be there for him even at his time of rest. I had to sit through the funeral service online. I felt helpless since I couldn't hug my mother and be there for my siblings.

In many ways, seeing it all made me want to die on the inside, particularly as they lowered the coffin into the grave and began tossing sand over the casket. It's difficult to fathom the gamut of emotions I was experiencing. It felt like I was streaming a dreadful and sad movie with a very poor signal at that. My dad's funeral had terrible Wi-Fi, and I kept losing connection. I do find some solace in the fact that I talked to him the day before he died. I had no idea my father would be proclaimed dead later that evening. We'd spoken about my writing a book about our family many times before. He was really proud of all of us. I just wish he'd lived long enough to read this book, which I've dedicated to him. I love you, Dad!

MICHAEL BANTU-KHOE

THE END!!!

MICHAEL
BANTU-KHOE

This is a watershed point in my life. For years, I have been looking for a way to describe my state of being to people. And now I am able to share it. I hope this inspires you to dig deep and find your empowering voice.

When I set out to write this book, I had just one goal in mind: to tell others about my background and how crazy my family and friends are. In retrospect, it was a challenging process, but I can confidently say that I am pleased I went through with it. When we start to look at the lives of others with compassion, we open ourselves up to a new world of understanding. Even when we can't change other people's behaviour, we can hope that someday they will change themselves for the better. The only one who can truly change us is us. If you want something different in your life, then make it happen! You can do it. Believe in yourself and never give up on yourself—you're amazing just as you are!

It is with heavy hearts that we announce the passing of our beloved father

Our Father

BORN   **DIED**

8 JUNE 1956 - 25 FEBRUARY 2021

Funeral service held on
3rd March, 9:00 AM

MICHAEL BANTU-KHOE

REVELATIONS 21: 3-4

3 With that I heard a loud voice from the throne say: "Look! The tent of God is with mankind, and he will reside with them, and they will be his people. And God himself will be with them. 4 And he will wipe out every tear from their eyes, and death will be no more, neither will mourning nor outcry nor pain be anymore. The former things have passed away."

OUR FATHER'S
LIFE JOURNEY

Baganetsi M, our King, was born on 8th June 1956, in the dusty Ngamiland village of Maun, to Tsalanang and the late Tshupelo M. He and his twin, Gaitsale M. had one younger brother, M. Marexg.

Our father's childhood journey started in 1965. He started his primary schooling at Thamalakane Primary School until 1971 and then continued to St Patrick Primary School where he completed in 1972. In 1973, he embarked on a journey to the south in search of knowledge and growth. He attended technical training at Madiba Builders Brigade between 1973 and 1975

MICHAEL BANTU-KHOE

1977 is the year that our father experienced the start of his working life when he was employed by Minestone Company in Francistown. The ever-faithful son of Maun returned home in May in 1977, where he worked for a veterinarian. In 1978 on the 15th of November our father joined the Botswana Defence Force after the historic Lesoma Tragedy that resulted in the massacre of 15 members of the newly-formed BDF. Upon successful completion of his training in 1979, he served in the BDF, based in Francistown.

A year later, in 1980, he met the love of his life Elva M. née Montsho. Theirs would be a strong and enduring union. On 28th September 1982, they were joined in holy matrimony and would celebrate 39 years of marriage. During this time, they were blessed with 12 children; these 12 disciples, as they are dubbed, have grown up to be the pillars who honour and cherish the family name.

He remained a member of the BDF until 2004 when he retired when he took up farming which would be his occupation until his departure from this world.

MICHAEL BANTU-KHOE

Our loving father was a devoted family man, a caring husband, doting grandfather, who was instrumental in making us who we are today. Our King leaves behind his wife, 12 children, 15 grandchildren, his mother and twin brother, four nieces, two nephews, two sons-in-law and three daughters in law.

We, the family, wish to express our sincerest gratitude to all those who have supported us during this time of loss. And to our father, we say, we will always value our King.

MICHAEL BANTU-KHOE

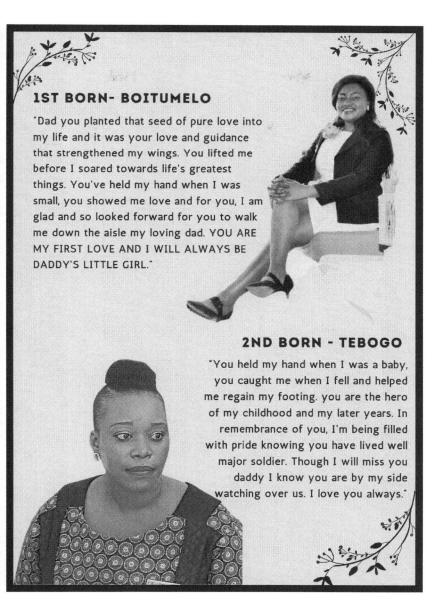

1ST BORN- BOITUMELO

"Dad you planted that seed of pure love into my life and it was your love and guidance that strengthened my wings. You lifted me before I soared towards life's greatest things. You've held my hand when I was small, you showed me love and for you, I am glad and so looked forward for you to walk me down the aisle my loving dad. YOU ARE MY FIRST LOVE AND I WILL ALWAYS BE DADDY'S LITTLE GIRL."

2ND BORN - TEBOGO

"You held my hand when I was a baby, you caught me when I fell and helped me regain my footing. you are the hero of my childhood and my later years. In remembrance of you, I'm being filled with pride knowing you have lived well major soldier. Though I will miss you daddy I know you are by my side watching over us. I love you always."

MICHAEL BANTU-KHOE

3RD BORN - THABISO

"When great leaders Fall. It emerges their heirs...who will step into their shoes n carry on their legacy. My father, you honoured your words to love and protect your family and planted a seed within us. I am who I am because of you. You were a pillar that induced strength in my life. I kneel down before you my King. I will forever honour and Uplift your name because you will forever live in our hearts. I know you can feel my tears, and you don't want me to cry but to be strong for our familyYet my heart is broken because a Stellar Man has gone. I pray that God will give me strength and somehow get me through as I struggle with the heartache that came when I lost you. Rest well Papa "

4TH BORN - THABO

To Dad,
No words can express how I feel but with God of Jacob, all is well. I love you and will always remember you.

MICHAEL BANTU-KHOE

5TH BORN - KEABETSWE HAZEL

"I will smile because you have lived, I will open my eyes and see all that you have left. I am full of the love that you shared, I am happy for tomorrow because of yesterday. I cherish your memory and will let it live. I will do what you would want: smile, open my eyes, love and be. I celebrate you and, this is not the end this is the continuation of life, you have been made alive in the spirit. Soldier on my hero, my dad. It's because if you I am."

6TH BORN - MICHAEL

"To my beloved father, you have always been loving and caring parent and I will forever treasure the memories we had together as father and son and with the whole family. I am the man I am today because of you. My biggest wish was for you to meet in person your grandson Isaac Thuso. But since you have gone too soon, I will be honored to tell him about you. About how happy and secure you made us all feel. You were and still are the head of our family. I love you papa, forever and forever and until we meet again."

MICHAEL BANTU-KHOE

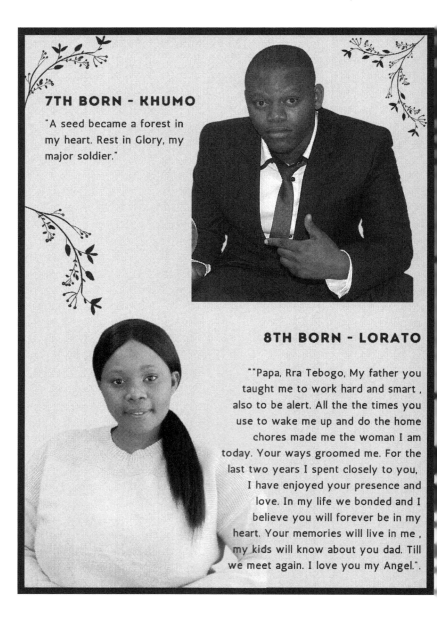

7TH BORN - KHUMO

"A seed became a forest in my heart. Rest in Glory, my major soldier."

8TH BORN - LORATO

""Papa, Rra Tebogo, My father you taught me to work hard and smart , also to be alert. All the the times you use to wake me up and do the home chores made me the woman I am today. Your ways groomed me. For the last two years I spent closely to you, I have enjoyed your presence and love. In my life we bonded and I believe you will forever be in my heart. Your memories will live in me , my kids will know about you dad. Till we meet again. I love you my Angel.".

MICHAEL BANTU-KHOE

9TH BORN - PHENYO

"What more can I ask for, you have journeyed with us and it's been perfect... Rest well Papa"

10TH BORN - NEO

"Dad I can't thank you enough for all you have done for me, you have always been a soldier, a hero, a teacher in my life. I am grateful for the time we spent together, but now i know there is a special Angel in heaven that is part of me. Its not where I wanted you to be but where God wanted you to be. keep well my Angel, I love you Papa"

MICHAEL BANTU-KHOE

11TH BORN - THATO

"A dad is someone who wants to catch you before you fall but instead pick you up, brushes you off and lets you try again. When I failed my form 5 you were hurt and I felt bad because I have failed you. So when I rewrote my form 5 I made sure that I'm going to make you proud. You were so happy and full of smiles when I passed my form 5 now I'm in university doing a course that I love. The last words u said to me were "O ithute fela thata o seka wa tshameka". With that, I will continue to make you proud Papa. I love you so much and I miss you more than ever. My look-alike"

12TH BORN - AKA LAST BORN TUMIE

"You will forever be my hero and I will forever cherish the love and care you gave me dad."

MICHAEL BANTU-KHOE

MICHAEL BANTU-KHOE

MICHAEL BANTU-KHOE

MICHAEL BANTU-KHOE

BLACK O'CLOCK PUBLISHING ®

MICHAEL BANTU-KHOE

in Michael Bantu-Khoe

@michaelban2khoe

@michaelban2khoe

@michaelban2khoe

Michael Ban2khoe

@michaelban2khoe

@michaelban2khoe

michaelban2khoe.com

Printed in Great Britain
by Amazon

83811826R00185